To my loving Mother, for gently guiding me on this journey of life but allowing me the space to find my own wings.

Contents

Chapter 1

My Dad was Magic

I don't have any memories of my mum or playing with my siblings when I was a young child, however, I do have lots of memories of my dad. I guess my brain knew to cherish those memories.

I have clear memories of my dad walking me and my siblings to school; my younger brother just a baby in a pram. Dad would take turns to lift me, my twin sister and my older sister, two years my senior, over the giant puddle that blocked our walking route to school. I remember waiting my turn whilst Dad carried my sisters first, rain dripping over my hood and into my eyes; it was cold and miserable, but it didn't matter because I had my super dad. Dad would often take us to the shop and buy us each a penny chew after collecting my older siblings from school. I remember watching him pick up the sweets and turning his back to me to pay the cashier; I remember looking at the back of his white pinstriped shirt that I haven't seen anyone wear since and feeling so much love and admiration for him. I was so naively secure at that time; life without Dad wasn't a thought that had ever crossed my mind, but why would it at three years old?

My dad was magic. He used to sit us all on his knee, and we would watch in amazement as he made the hanky disappear and reappear, again and again and again. My favourite magic trick was the one he would do with our school bookbags; looking back now, all he used to do was open and close it, but somehow he made it look like it was magic. I remember happiness, natural, effortless happiness.

I have clear memories of Dad in his wheelchair; I would sit on his knee and cuddle in to his chest. Dad was never a skinny man so he was extra warm and extra comfy to snuggle in to. I never did question why Dad started having to use a wheelchair; I was a lazy child so I mostly just appreciated that I could sit on his knee instead of having to walk.

I remember parts of our last family holiday with Dad as if it were yesterday; we visited a dinosaur museum and I was sitting on Dad's knee in the wheelchair when he lifted me up and pretended to throw me to the dinosaurs. I felt utterly betrayed – 'How could my dad do this to me?' – and, worse still, Dad laughed whilst I cried my eyes out. I was confused as to why Dad would laugh when I was so upset. I was traumatised yet again on this holiday when we were at an evening children's show and there was a pretend wrestling match. I did not want to leave my dad's side. However, my siblings and our new friends wanted to get closer to the wrestling ring, and I didn't want to be singled out so I went with them. I remember looking back as I walked away and a feeling of dread at the pit of my stomach. I tried to enjoy the show like my siblings were but barely five minutes into it, one of the wrestlers made a roaring noise and pulled a scary face. Without a second thought, I turned and I ran! I remember crying my eyes out, running through what felt like hundreds of giant legs. For a moment I couldn't see Dad; I was filled with dread and fear. Finally I spotted him. He was looking straight at me; he was laughing at me again but this time I didn't care, I just wanted to get to him as fast as I could. He scooped me up into his arms and cradled me as I wept. I remember my relief; safe at last! Looking back, I know my dad did not take his eyes off me for one moment; he likely anticipated my reaction and made sure he was ready to scoop me up. I know Dad loved the opportunity to hold me close and rescue me as much as I loved him doing it; he was my safe place.

I have memories of hearing my dad fall down the stairs and the ambulance taking him away. I'm not sure if they were linked or separate events but I know my mum did a good job of reassuring me because I didn't feel worried at this time. I started to feel something was strange when Dad's bed moved into the living room. He had a pink curtain around the bed; I didn't understand this then but of course now I know this was so he was able to have some privacy. I remember feeling shy, not knowing what to do with myself when I saw Dad lying in this bed. He smiled and showed me how I could play toy cars on his belly whilst he was lying in the bed. Even at only five years old, I knew that this was my dad's attempt to reassure me so I decided to play along. My younger brother and I pushed the cars up and over Dad's big belly; my brother was thoroughly enjoying this game but something did not feel right to me. I believe this was the first time I realised something was wrong with my daddy.

On the 8th August 1996, Dad passed away within one year of being diagnosed with a brain stem tumour. He left behind his three-year-old son, five-year-old twin daughters, seven-year-old daughter, fifteen-year-old daughter, seventeen-year-old son and my mum.

A Child's Grief

I am in church with my family and lots of other people; I am cold. Everyone around me is sad. I look to my twin sister who is standing next to me and she is really sad; I have never seen her cry so much. I know she is crying for my dad; am I a bad person because I am not sad? I must cry. I begin to force tears so that I am crying like my sister.

I distinctly remember the coffin being lowered into the ground and watching my mum throw soil over it, and then the priest handing me the soil. I copied as my mum had done, and threw the soil. I remember wanting to do it as quickly as possible to avoid people looking at me for too long, like we had all done with my mum. I knew something bad had happened; I knew it involved my dad but I didn't know what it was.

As the years went by, I continued to question that day and, mostly, where my dad had gone. I don't remember exactly when I had the thoughts and actions I'm about to share with you, but I know they were between the ages of five and twelve years old and in this order:

- Where is my dad? Is every man in my life just going to disappear? Now I feel sad. I cry every time a man leaves the room.
- I look for my dad everywhere: in the shop, in the park and out of the car window.
- I write a secret letter to my dad and throw it out of my bedroom window. The next morning, I see it wet and crumpled on the road. I choose to ignore it and believe my letter got to Dad; I wait for Dad's response.
- I fantasise about opening the living room door on Christmas morning and seeing Dad sitting in the armchair.
- I fantasise about Dad with a new family, in a big posh house in London. I wait for him to come back to get me.
- I fantasise that Dad had to go to some far away country to help find the cure for his illness. I wait for him to come home with the cure.

I can't remember when I eventually understood my dad's death and what his death meant, but I remember the day I accepted that he was not coming home. I was around twelve years old; we were on a family holiday. My twin sister was playing with one of those flour-filled balloons. I was looking out of the car window for my dad. My sister's balloon burst and the flour went everywhere. In that very moment, I realised my dad was not coming home.

Chapter 2

Dad's Visit

During my secondary school years, I didn't think about Dad too much. Mum's new partner had moved into our home and I was satisfied that I had a father figure in my life. I was popular at school and my focus was mostly on my girlfriends, hair, make-up, underage drinking and boys. The transition to college at seventeen years old, however, proved challenging. I missed the structure and routine of school, and I had no idea what I wanted to do with my life. Growing up felt scary and my mood became very low. I lost a lot of self-confidence and I isolated myself from my family and friends. It was during this time that my sister told me about a close friend of hers who had recovered from cancer, and who had found comfort in her belief of Angels. Shortly after this conversation with my sister, I was doing my usual morning chores, and I was about to turn on the vacuum cleaner, when I was drawn to the television; I had 'This Morning' on and the presenters were questioning a lady called Lorna Byrne who claimed to see Angels in her everyday life. I was initially quite sceptical, however curiosity got the better of me and I bought her book, 'Angels in my Hair'. I can't remember what made me buy the book or even having it delivered, but I do know this book really transformed my life; it opened up my mind to the possibility of the afterlife and mystical beings. Something Lorna really encourages you to do in her books is to listen to that quiet little voice within; she says that is your Guardian Angel guiding you to make the right choices. That little voice within saved me from becoming very sick.

I was on the bus home from college when, out of nowhere, I felt a quiet little voice within tell me to get off the bus at my local medical practice and go in and tell the nurse I had not been feeling well, and I had lost a lot of weight. Almost as if I was in a trance, I did as the voice said without a second thought. It was the evening walk-in clinic and so I got an appointment with Nurse Archibald there and then. The nurse gasped when I stood on the weighing scales. I am naturally petite and have never weighed more than seven and a half stone so I really didn't have much weight on me to lose, but at a time where everything seemed to be out of my control, I found comfort in controlling my food intake, and hadn't realised that this was becoming an unhealthy obsession. We all find strange ways of coping when we are going through a crisis, and normally it involves abusing our bodies: drugs, alcohol, self-harm, sex, exercising too much or not at all, eating too much or not at all, etc. I was becoming deficient in vitamins; I was tired all the time but I could not sleep and, consequently, I was irritable and I was struggling to concentrate at college. The strange thing is, even though I did as that little voice within told me, I genuinely had no idea that I was unwell at that time; in fact, I remember thinking I was healthier than ever because I only ate fruit and vegetables.

It is proven that eating disorders have the best outcome when caught early, and so I do believe that if I had not listened to that little voice within and sought help when I did, I would have got really quite sick. Consequently, I would not have been able to achieve the grades to get into university and the opportunities I have today may not have been available to me. Likewise, if I had not sought that appointment at that exact time, I may have been allocated a different nurse who may not have had the same impact on my recovery as Nurse Archibald. It took me around ten months to regain the weight I had lost in the three months I had been unwell. Nurse Archibald would weigh me every week; although this sounds intrusive, I always enjoyed the appointments because she was such a joy to be around; she was like a warm cup of tea on a cold winter's day. Nurse Archibald was often my motivation to gain the weight. She would celebrate with me when I gained a few kilos, and although she never degraded me for not gaining weight, or the few occasions when I lost weight, I knew she cared that I got better and I did not want to let her down.

Nurse Archibald is a wonderful example of the impact we have on other people's lives. My appointments with her were only once a week for ten minutes and I imagine she was nothing but herself, but that was enough to have a real positive impact on my life because herself was so pure and kind. This is why it is very important to be kind to everyone you meet because you never know what they are going through and you never know the impact you can have on their life.

My new found connection to Angels was another important factor to my recovery. I began acknowledging my Guardian Angel in my mind every day; I would ask it for help with things like doing my college work, directions, finding things I had lost, and to help uplift me when I was having a bad day. I found that the more I asked the Angels for help, the stronger that little voice within would get. For example, I would be guided to a paragraph in a book that would inform my assessment and I have a very poor sense of direction so I would often get anxious when going somewhere new on my own because I always got lost, but I was getting lost a lot less. That little voice within was guiding me in the right direction. The more this was happening, the more help I would ask for, and the more confident I would become in my belief that Angels do exist. I did not need to see my Guardian Angel to know it was there; the coincidences that I was experiencing in my daily life since acknowledging the Angels were enough for me to believe. However, I would be allowed to see my Guardian Angel in form just over ten years later.

Lorna Byrne's book encouraged my connection to the Angels, which opened my mind to spirituality and the possibility of communicating with my dad in Spirit; had I not had that conversation with my sister, had I not chosen to put 'This Morning' on the TV or to buy the book, all of the experiences I share in this book may not have been. My belief in Angels would be the very beginning of an incredibly magical journey and a connection to my dad like no other. Although the Angels are not the focus of this book, I felt it important to acknowledge where my journey began.

During this time, my dad visited me in a dream for the first time since his passing. I don't recall seeing my dad but I do remember being in a bright white space, feeling my dad's presence, and hearing his voice say, "*Don't worry, I have chosen you to be my Angel.*" When I woke up and reflected on the dream, I believed he was telling me I was going to die, because Angels are dead, right? When I shared this with my mum, she laughed it off and suggested the dream was simply linked to the books I had been reading. I struggled to accept this as Dad felt so real in the dream, and why hadn't I ever dreamt of him before?

Whilst I have never forgotten this dream, I didn't think about it too much. After my period of being unwell, I found a new love for life. I was experiencing a mini awakening; I was becoming aware of the magic that surrounds me every day. I was connecting to my Guardian Angel on a deeper level and I even began to become aware of the other Angels that surround us. I felt safe, guided and protected. Life became so much easier. I realised aspirations to work in Children's Services. I got into university, achieved multiple qualifications to Masters' level, met the love of my life and got (what I thought was) my dream job by the time I was twenty-eight years old.

Throughout these years, I began to think about Dad more; I figured that if I was able to have communication with my Guardian Angel, Dad too could communicate with me and guide me, just as my Guardian Angel had been. Initially, it was difficult for me to distinguish the difference between my Guardian Angel's energy and my dad's energy and this could be frustrating. However, Dad found ways of helping me to recognise his energy and, for many years, I relied on the signs he would send me. Today I do not rely on signs from Dad so much as I can clearly recognise his energy, but this took almost ten years of personal and spiritual growth. From around nineteen years old, I began speaking to Dad in my mind almost every day. I asked him and the Angels to help me with many things like passing my law exam and driving test, as well as succeeding at job interviews. I cried to him some days like when I broke up with boyfriends, and when I failed my driving test for the third time, or when it felt unfair that I didn't have my dad here when I needed him. Dad didn't answer me, at least not as I would have liked him to at that time.

Love Hearts and Cologne

Whilst Dad didn't visit me in a dream again for many years, or directly answer the questions I asked him in my mind, he found other ways to reassure me he was hearing me. I started to notice love hearts. Everywhere I looked there seemed to be heart shapes: in the clouds, in puddles on the floor, steam on the bathroom mirror would be in the shape of a heart; I didn't know so many companies used love hearts to promote their products. At first I didn't think much of this, but it was happening so often that I couldn't ignore it. And then one night I was lying in bed and a strong smell of cologne came out of nowhere. It was so strong I sat up and searched my bedroom for where it could be coming from. I wasn't in a relationship at the time and hadn't had a man in my bedroom for a long time so I was totally baffled and a little freaked out. The smell faded but reappeared several times within a few months and seemed to follow me around. I was living between university accommodation and my mum's home at the time, and it would appear on an evening in both bedrooms as I was relaxed and getting ready to go to sleep. I would go crazy trying to source the smell; I would get my flat mates and family members in my bedroom, and I would ask if they could smell it. They never could. One day, Mum very casually said to me, "*Your dad used to always wear cologne.*" As I considered this, the smell reappeared and I was drawn to a stone the shape of a love heart on the ground.

When you realise Spirit communication, you are given instant clarification by way of 'energy feels': you might go hot or cold; you may get a shiver down your back or tingles all over your head and down your shoulders and arms. This is Spirit thanking you for acknowledging them. This is what I felt that day when I finally realised where the cologne and love hearts were coming from. The energy feels were very subtle for me at first but have developed substantially since I have learnt to acknowledge my dad, Angels and Spirit. For a few years, I relied on the physical signs. I would ask my dad to send me a love heart as a sign or bright white feathers. He always sent them.

One morning I was out on a walk. I had planned to walk my favourite fell, Latrigg, but I spontaneously decided to change route and visit my dad's grave. I asked Dad in my mind to send me a white feather as a sign that he was there. I busied myself at Dad's grave, re-arranging the flowers my older sister had laid for him days earlier, brushing soil from his headstone, talking to him in my mind as I was doing so. Amongst all of this, I had forgotten about my request to Dad. I touched his gravestone for a moment as I always do before I leave, and I began the short walk to leave the graveyard. There are four gates that can be used to enter and leave the graveyard, but in the ten years I had been visiting Dad's grave, I always used the same gate. As I was walking towards the gate, I had a feeling that I should leave out of the other gate which would add an extra minute to my walk so I changed direction. I noted that there was a beautiful white flowering tree that I had never paid much attention to before, when a brilliant white feather floated down and gently swayed in front of my face and down to my feet. It was so white, it was practically glowing. I took a picture of it laid on the floor at my feet before picking it up and placing it in my pocket. This is not the first or last time Dad has done this for me, but it never feels any less magical. That feeling I had to change my walking route and to use the other gate was my dad communicating with me through my intuition; he was linking his energy into my energy to guide me, just like our Guardian Angels do. Dad had probably set this up before I even began my walk, knowing that I would ask for the feather and that this would brighten my day and enhance my belief in Spirit, magic and him. As humans, we are taught that communication should be something we hear or see; we are not encouraged to communicate through feel. Some mediums do see and hear Spirit but generally Spirit will communicate through feel because they do not have physical form anymore. Have you ever heard anyone say listen to your heart or listen to your gut? They don't mean physically – they mean listen to the energy of your heart. How many times have you said, *"I've got a good feeling about this"* or *"I knew I shouldn't have done that"*? The more you listen to your feelings, the more likely you are to make the right choices and the stronger your intuition will become. How do you think your body knew you shouldn't have done that before it even happened? It might just be that someone in Spirit was communicating that information with you through feel, and guiding you to make the right choice.

As I continued to talk to my dad in my mind and acknowledge his presence, he found more creative ways to communicate with me. I was out for a run listening to 'Running Music Hits UK' on Spotify when I heard a loud whistle in my left ear. I got the fright of my life and quickly turned around expecting someone to be standing behind me; needless to say I was a little unnerved when no one was there. I told my mum about this and she said, *"Your dad used to whistle all the time.*" This reminded me of a conversation I had with a local lady who told me that she used to call my dad 'Mr Whistle' because he was always whistling. A few days later, I was cleaning the bathroom when I heard the whistle again. It was so loud and clear that I had to search the house to check I was definitely home alone. I berated Dad in my mind for scaring the life out of me again, before smiling and thanking him for visiting me. One of the most beautiful forms of communication from Dad to me is through music; it all began when my partner and I were on holiday and I was a little restless as I was waiting to hear if I had been successful for a job application. Two days into the holiday I received an email. The time zones were different so I received the email at around ten p.m. I hid in the bathroom to read it and was disheartened to find that my application was unsuccessful. I cried and sheepishly got back into bed whilst my partner slept. The next morning, I woke up to the song 'I Just Called To Say I Love You' by Stevie Wonder going around and around in my head. I hadn't heard this song for a long time and it wasn't one of my favourite songs, so I thought it strange that it should spontaneously enter my mind. I was getting better at recognising my dad's energy by now, and so I soon realised this song was sent from him to cheer me up, and it certainly did. I shared this experience with my eldest sister who has a lot more memories of life with Dad on earth, and she couldn't believe it; she said this song reminds her of Dad because it was always playing in the pub he managed. I had never linked that song to Dad before this experience and have no memories of Dad playing that song when I was a child. This was wonderful verification, and further encouraged my belief that Dad was finding ways to communicate with me from Heaven.

Dad's Face in the Wall

I was still at a time in my life where I believed the most valid way Dad could show me there is life after death would be to allow me to physically see him again. I would ask all the time to see his face again. One morning, I woke up and decided to relax in bed before rising. I was looking ahead of me and gradually I saw a face in the wall appear; it was Dad smiling like a Cheshire cat. I got the fright of my life. I jumped out of bed and then he was gone. Initially I knew it was him but, as time passed, I began to believe less and less. I told myself I was probably tired and seeing things (though I had never 'seen things' when I was tired before). A few months later, a very good friend of mine asked if I would go to see a renowned medium with her. I agreed. My friend had the first sitting. She told me later that the medium asked if she knew a gentleman named Billy. She said no and so he carried on with his reading. The medium asked again, *"Are you sure you don't know a gentleman named Billy? He is very persistent."* Again my friend said no. When it was my turn, the medium said, *"Do you know a gentleman named Billy? He is desperately trying to connect to his daughter."* I smiled and explained that this was my dad. He said, *"You talk to him in your mind every day; he wants you to know that he can hear you.*" And then he said he is singing the song 'You'll Never Walk Alone.' My immediate interpretation of this was that Dad was telling me that he will always walk beside me and guide me. However, when I shared this with my mum, she explained that this was the song that was played at Dad's funeral (my dad was Liverpudlian). This medium also delivered messages from my dad to each of my siblings; this was accurate to the point that he was able to describe items that my sister had bought when shopping days earlier, and clothes my brother had taken to the launderette. Towards the end of the reading, the medium said, *"You have seen your dad since his passing; he was smiling at you."* As he said this a vision of Dad smiling like a Cheshire cat came in to my mind and I was instantly reminded of his face in the wall.

I berated myself for a while for not believing in Dad's visual visit and for feeling frightened when I did. He's definitely not going to show himself to me again now, I thought. It takes a lot of energy for a Spirit to manifest their human form; imagine going to all that effort for your loved one to run away or freeze in fear. Aside from the disappointment, this would upset the Spirit person as they would never wish to scare their loved ones. This is a reason why Spirits don't often show themselves in human form to family members. They may appear as a robin, a feather, a song or something that their loved one will recognise as significant to their deceased family member. We are more likely to react with love and joy when we experience these things than if we see a Spirit in human form. People may say, *"I would never act* scared if I saw my deceased husband/parent/child/sibling, etc. in human form; I would be overjoyed." Perhaps some people would be overjoyed, but the majority would freak out because we are taught that we are not supposed to see dead people. Children are more in tune with their spiritual side. I have heard people say that this is because they are fresh from Heaven, and they are not as conditioned by humanity as teenagers and adults are.

My older sister has always spoken about Dad to her children; they know him as Grandad Billy. When they were very young, they would go to visit his grave and they would look up to the sky and sing to Grandad Billy in Heaven. I have always sensed that my youngest niece had spiritual abilities and therefore I had anticipated her to open up about this at some point but I didn't expect her to say what she did. My two nieces and I were watching a movie, when my youngest niece said, "I saw Grandad Billy in my bedroom." When I asked what he was doing there, she said he was just standing there, looking at her and smiling. She said she knew it was him because of the photo her mum has of him. I thanked my niece for sharing this with me and we had a brief discussion about how she feels about this and what she could do if she does not wish to see Spirit. It is very important that we do not act scared when children tell us such stories about seeing deceased loved ones as this may worry or upset the child, and there really is no need to fear; rather, it is a beautiful gift and reassurance that their loved ones are still watching over them.

Chapter 3

Strengthening My Connection to Dad and Beyond

I can't pinpoint when I began having a stronger connection to Dad and other Spiritual Beings, it just happened over time. I do believe that acknowledging Dad and all the signs he was sending me strengthened his connection to me. If we want to connect to higher realms, we can't just sit there and expect it to happen: we need to meet Spirit half way. This means we need to, at the very least, acknowledge the signs our loved ones in Heaven are sending us and more so we need to work on ourselves; we need to nurture our spiritual self and increase our energy frequency. A number of significant events have happened throughout my life thus far that have encouraged my personal and spiritual growth and ultimately enhanced my connection to Dad, Angels and other Spirit. These events include: the loss of my dad when I was a young child, the eating disorder when I was seventeen, finding Lorna Byrne's books, a romantic relationship, the sudden death of a loved one, animal rescues and discovering reiki energy healing. All of these circumstances have encouraged me to look within, to self-analyse, to heal, to forgive, to love unconditionally and to become self-aware.

These circumstances in my life enabled me to unearth emotional baggage that was weighing me down, bring it to the forefront, learn from it and heal. There will always be emotional baggage throughout our lifetime on earth, but how we view the emotional baggage is what can weigh us down if we are not careful. For the most part, I have learnt to embrace the emotional baggage and to be grateful for the lessons it has come to teach me. However, some days are more challenging than others. Over the years, I have realised that I have strong intuition: this means Angels, Spirit and my dad can communicate with me through my intuition. Rather than physically seeing or hearing Dad, I feel his words. I used to give out to Spirit and ask that they allow me to see and hear more. I believed that I had to see it or hear it to believe it, but I am now very grateful that Spirit predominantly communicates with me through feel; I would really think I was going mad if I was seeing and hearing as much as I feel. I talk about *feel* a lot in this book: I do not mean to physically feel but to feel energetically. Another term I could use is '*Being*'. Spirit communicates to me through a state of Being. Spirit has since taught me that to communicate through *feel* or *Being* is the highest, truest form of communication and that highly evolved beings communicate solely through feel. I have learnt that when Dad communicates with me, I mostly feel him on my left side.

We can give Spirit calling cards which will help us to understand who is visiting and what message they want to deliver. For example, if it's Grandad, I get the energy feels in my right hand. However, as we are all individual and unique, not everyone will be as sensitive to feel as I am. Others may be more aware of smell, or seeing, so they may have a specific smell or colour as a calling card. I don't really use calling cards anymore as I am able to feel the energy of the loved one that is visiting me and to distinguish the difference. It is very hard to explain but through my ability to feel so strongly, I can see and hear through what I am feeling.

Throughout the book, I refer to visions a lot: some of these visions are visual where I seem to be transported to another place, but many of them are visions that are not visual as such but they are visions that are played out through feel. I find this a much gentler way to communicate with Spirit; although I do occasionally see and hear Spirit, I choose not to exercise this as much as I could.

I could never have imagined that receiving feathers from Dad as verification of his unlimited existence would evolve to the level it has now, where I have been allowed to see Dad in my mind's eye and cuddle him in my dreams. But it was not only Dad that would communicate with me. As you delve further into the book, I share communication and visual visits from other people in Spirit, from animals in Spirit, and from an energy that some call 'God'.

God

I have come a long way since I began typing this book in November 2020. I had no intention of writing about God, but in the end I was guided to include a chapter and the idea was that it would be at the end of the book. I planned for this chapter to be short and sweet but, as I began typing, I couldn't stop. A passionate, excited energy arose within me and the words just kept flowing. I was happy with this one chapter – I had divulged more than I had originally planned to, but as it was done, I felt OK about it. Spirit gently nudged me to include more about God in the book but I tried my hardest to ignore them. As I so often proofread my book, I felt a nag in the pit of my stomach. I had originally left so much of God's guidance out. I knew I was not only doing my experiences a disservice but I was leaving so much truth out. I knew that this book could never have the impact I would like it to if I was not at least ninety-five per cent open about my experiences; I have chosen not to share the experiences that Spirit have not encouraged me to share, that is the five percent that I am keeping to myself for now. Whilst my experiences with Dad is a predominant factor in this book, I learnt that the inspiration behind the name 'A Father's Love' means so much more than I had originally thought.

My connection with Dad and Spirit was growing stronger but I never really gave God much thought at all. I was raised Catholic,

Christian until I was around thirteen years old when my mum let me choose if I wanted to continue to attend church and I chose not to. So, I had a perception of God but I wasn't sure I believed in it. My only real memory of church (other than physically being there) was when I was confirmed at around eleven years old. As a part of confirmation in the Catholic Church, we are asked to choose a Saint's name; it is believed that this is the Saint who will serve as a special patron to protect and guide the individual who bears their name. When my mum asked me who I would like to choose as my Saint, I immediately knew who I would choose because I'd had a beautiful experience only weeks earlier.

As a child, I found church quite boring and I never really listened, however, during this particular service something drew me in when the priest was sharing the story of Mother Teresa; I remember being in awe of this Saint I had never heard of before. I was completely engrossed. I thought to myself, *'That is what I want to be. I want to help people like Mother Teresa did.'* And then I was overcome by the most beautiful energy. It surrounded the whole of my body in the most loving embrace, and it made me feel that this is exactly what I would do – I am important, I am protected and I will have an impact on this earth. I have never forgotten this experience. Anytime I would feel sad as a child or worried about school in my teenage years, I would remember this energy and I would instantly feel at ease knowing that I would be safe no matter what.

I have never spoken to anyone about this experience; I'm not sure why I chose not to because I am very close with my siblings and my mum. I had always thought it was perhaps something everyone experiences at some point in their life. I still believe it is something everyone experiences, for I am certain we are all important, protected and destined to have an impact on this earth. The difference being, I remembered the experience. I'm not sure everyone else does.

In my late twenties, I began to have experiences which encouraged my connection to God and, to this day, there is no doubt in my mind that God exists. I recognise God as He because God presents to me as a loving father; that does not mean God is male or a parental figure but it means that this is my predominant perception of God. I have spoken to Christians who have experienced God as a female despite their religion teaching them God is male. I don't believe God has a sex or a form of any kind. I believe God is infinite and everything, and I believe God will present as whatever we need Him to be at any given time. For example, for many years I felt I was missing out on the father-daughter bond, even though I had a loving and supportive step-dad. I chose to feel lack and I always craved the special relationship that I believed only daughters and birth fathers could have. For many years I had an idealism of the perfect father in my mind, when in reality that did not exist in my birth dad or my step-dad. However, in my experiences with God which I discuss in more detail later in the book, He presents as the perfect father and everything I ever wished a father to be. Yet, for another person, God may present as a loving mother, a child, an animal, a feeling, light, a colour, a rainbow and so on. God also does not identify with a name. I use the term God, Universe and Source throughout the book. They all refer to the same energy.

When you experience a spiritual awakening, whether you believe in God as a father, as an energy, as the Universe, etc. you will experience a connection to God because you have acknowledged your Truth within, which is ultimately God/Source/Consciousness/the Universe (whatever you want to call it), and so you will find that you become a more compassionate and loving person. You may not even believe in a God but, as you become more aware of your Truth and your power within, you are acknowledging God within you because your Eternity, your Soul, is derived from Source. God and Spirit communicate to me via three methods: predominantly through feel – people who have hearing loss will have a very good understanding of this method of communication as I believe that they 'hear' people through vibrations/feel. So when I write, 'God said, without words,' I mean God is saying through feel or vibration. Secondly, God communicates to me via visions. This is when I am directly in God's presence and the communication is verbal – I can hear God's words. This is my favourite method of communicating with God as I feel His love intensified, and I am my spiritual self in the visions which is much more freeing. Thirdly, God communicates to me through my thoughts. I know when a thought comes from God or Spirit because the words are beautiful and the knowledge is wise. It will be repeated in my mind over and over again until I acknowledge it. For example, when my self-esteem was very low during my eating disorder at seventeen, I would wake up in the morning to a thought that would say, '*I love you, I love you so much*' over and over again. This happened every morning and I would think it strange that I was saying that to myself in my mind. When I found Lorna Byrne's book, I eventually acknowledged that this thought – '*I love you*' – was coming from my Guardian Angel and then it stopped. I asked Spirit how I would know if my thoughts were coming from Source or from myself (my ego). Spirit said that any thought that is beautiful and evokes feelings of calm and peace comes from Source; any thought that is upsetting or hurtful comes from the ego. It's that simple.

For over a year I was confused about my newfound connection to God, especially as I had not actively sought God and I was no longer following a religion. However, as I have written this book, I have found out that many people have had experiences with God in recent years – people who follow a religion and people who do not follow a religion. I believe that God is reaching out to humankind because we are at a crucial time in human evolution, and the choices we make today determine the fate of humankind and all life on earth. "*What is it that God wants us to do?*" you ask. The answer is very simple: choose love.

I am learning so much about God and my perception of God has changed since I began writing A Father's Love. There is still a lot of unknowns about God, not least how His energy came in to existence but Spirit always remind me that God is not complicated and that I must trust in the glimpses of God that I am given, and God's wish for me to share my experiences in this book. There is knowledge that I know to be absolute truth, such as God's incredible love for humankind and God's wishes to be accepted and loved by humankind, and there is information that I have experienced but my understanding has or will change over time. I trust that this is OK too – sometimes what we believe to be true at one time is true at that time but is no longer true at another time, because our awareness and knowledge has changed.

I was over halfway through typing this book when I realised the connection to the name of the book and my perception of God as a loving father. Spirit had chosen not to divulge this information to me any sooner than they did because they knew that I may well have chosen not to type the book. I was confused and very secretive about my experiences with God at the time. I was scared that I would offend people and lose people I love. The only way they were going to convince me to start this book was to type about my experiences with Dad.

Chapter 4

My First Love

Richard John Honey (known as 'Dick') was my first ever love. I was two years old and he was around sixty-five years my senior. I remember my mum was ironing in the living room when I told her: *"I'm going to marry Grandad."* I loved my grandad with every piece of my tiny heart; he was my favourite place to be. My mum told me that when she found out she was pregnant with my twin sister and me, my grandad said to her, *"You have given me what I have always wanted"*. Mum said he used to love it when my sister and I would walk around holding hands and when we would get up to mischief, like helping one another climb out of the crib and covering our faces in Mum's make-up. I believe my grandad was one in a million. He was an exceptionally kind, loving and compassionate man. Looking back, I find it quite profound that in just two years of life, I developed so much love for my grandad. I was a shy child but, when I was with Grandad, I was a social butterfly. I would talk and talk and talk, and he would just smile and listen. I knew how much he loved me; I believe that's why I felt safe to express myself when I was with him. I know my parents loved me dearly but they had five other children and they both worked very hard, so it was often a fight to get their undivided attention. I loved to have Grandad to myself, my grandma would walk ahead with my baby brother and my sisters, and Grandad would stay by me whilst I dawdled behind. Of course, I knew exactly what I was doing and I think Grandad probably did too. Grandad had fifteen other grandchildren but I don't remember ever feeling like I had to fight for his attention. In fact, I always felt he loved me the most, though I'm sure he made my siblings and cousins feel equally as loved. I remember my older cousins tormenting me, asking me questions that a three-year-old could never answer. I cuddled into Grandad as he whispered the answers to me. I remember one of the questions they asked was, *"Who is our Prime Minister?"* And I misheard Grandad's whisper. I don't know what I said but it was obviously funny because they all started laughing at me. I hid my head in Grandad's shoulder as he gently told my cousins to leave me alone.

Grandad was a typical green-fingered Grandad and I would often sit in the greenhouse with him whilst he tended to his plants, or we would look at the fish in his pond. I vividly remember busying myself with a toy wheelbarrow whilst my grandad was working in the garden. I can't imagine I left Grandad's side very much at all when we were visiting my grandparents. I remember watching Grandad stirring a cup of tea; he would really give it a good stir and so occasionally I do that now to try to take myself back to my grandparents' kitchen.

My grandad was very clever. He had been a respected pilot with the Royal Air Force, a maths and science teacher, and a headteacher. He was a skilled handyman in almost everything; he had made my eldest sister a doll's house and he had knitted my other older sister a blanket. It wasn't long before I stole the blanket and adopted it as my own. I guess it smelt of Grandad. I lost it many times and when I was much younger I would scream the house down until it was found, so much so I would disturb the neighbours and they would kindly help my mum look for it. I called it 'cuddly' and I had it until I was fourteen years old. My memories of Grandad are very limited but one thing I remember very, very well is the incredible love we had for one another.

My grandparents were told that they were genetically incompatible and would never have children, however, five years into their marriage, they fell pregnant with my uncle John; they were told he was a miracle baby and they would not have any more children. Following the birth of uncle John, my grandparents had another five healthy miracle babies almost consecutively. I guess that makes my cousins, and siblings and I miracle grandchildren since medical science said we were never supposed to be here. As I reflect on my grandad's loving patience and his smiling eyes, I believe he was grateful every day for his children and grandchildren and, for most of his life, he couldn't believe his luck.

My grandad passed away suddenly the day before my dad was diagnosed with the brain stem tumour. I remember dreaming of Grandad after he passed away. We were in a very busy room full of relatives, some I knew and some I did not. Everyone was so happy and excited; they seemed to be having a party. I knew my grandad had passed away and I found the whole thing confusing and overwhelming. Now I know this was Grandad's 'welcome home' party.

My grandad had a soft smile that would light up the kindness in his eyes. When I take myself back to it, it feels like a warm hug. Many people look for particular physical qualities in a romantic partner, but I did not care much for those; I looked for someone who had the same kindness that my grandad had. I did not find this for many years, and my yearning for this, and lack of it in romantic relationships, caused a lot of pain and disappointment. Eventually I stopped looking for Grandad's kindness and accepted this quality was unique only to him.

My Wish Letter

It was just after Christmas, and I was visiting my hometown for a few weeks before going back to university. I decided to stay an extra week so that I could be with my family on my twenty-second birthday. My brother asked me to attend a promotion he was doing for a product at the gym he worked at; I was very into my fitness at the time, so I was more than happy to go along. Whilst there, I bumped in to a friend and I mentally noted that he was sitting next to a very attractive young man. I was surprised when he introduced this man as his older brother because they were a local family and I thought I knew just about everybody in my area. I commented to the attractive man that I had not seen him before and his response was a simple smile. His smile evoked something within me. I thought about it for longer than I liked to at that time as I was intent on staying clear of men to focus on my university studies. I returned to my university accommodation a few days later. Caught up in the whirlwind of assessment deadlines, my dissertation and lots of partying, I soon forgot about him.

Around six months later, I graduated university and I moved back in with my mum. I decided I would like to settle down and find a loving relationship but this didn't happen as quickly as I thought it would. I went on many dates but they never felt right. This was getting me down as I had been the only single person at a few family weddings I had attended at that time. I can't remember why I decided to do what I did as I had never done anything like this since the incident where I found my letter to Dad crumpled on the road, but I decided to write a wish letter to my dad. Within the letter I asked that he would sprinkle some magic on me and send me a man who would be faithful and true. Of course, I didn't post the letter. I read it out loud only once, saved it to my laptop and didn't look at it again for two years.

I remember I genuinely didn't think any magic would happen; I actually forgot about the letter and went on with my life. Four months after I typed this letter it would be Christmas. One week before Christmas I bumped into my friend's attractive older brother in our local nightclub. We fell in love very quickly and we are still together seven years later. It would be many months into our relationship before I figured out what his smiled evoked within me on that day I had met him at the gym; it was the warm hug I had been yearning for, for all those years.

About two years into my relationship, I found the wish letter. I read it and I thought to myself: *'How pathetic Anne'*. To be honest I did think it a strange coincidence that I found my perfect man four months after typing that letter and during the most magical time of year, but I told myself that it was just that: a coincidence. Around four years into my relationship, I went to a psychic fair and had my Tarot cards read. The lady was very good; she spoke about my relationship and what was going on in my life at that time but I really wanted guidance on my career. She was talking about how Spirit wanted me to write down my career goals and then she said: "*You need to make a wish, like you did with your partner.*"

I was guided to share this experience because Spirit wants you to know that there is such a thing as magic – we just need to know how to make a wish.

Wishes are essentially prayers; both are energies that you put out into the Universe and both are mostly asking for something. Wishing with all your heart is the same as praying with all your heart and, in both cases, the more you wish and the more heartfelt the wish is, the more likely it is to become true. I always say a prayer before I go to bed and Spirit have allowed me to see gold sparkles coming from me and going out into the Universe whilst I am praying. I am making my wish through that prayer; I am setting an intention and giving it out to the Universe, to God. The energy of my wish is created in that very moment.

I am not very good at expressing myself verbally but, when I start writing/typing, my words flow naturally. I find that answers come to me when I am writing. Likewise, I can express my desires or my wishes more clearly when writing them down. This is my creativity. Creativity is derived from the Soul and Soul work comes from the heart, so expressing a wish via our creativity enhances the wish. People's creativity may include singing, painting, dancing, etc. If you can focus on your wish whilst doing something that makes your Soul sing, you are greatly increasing the chances of your wish coming true exactly as it is destined to because it is coming from your Soul, which is your Truth, your spark of God within.

Gratitude is another great way to make sure your wish is heard loud and clear and also gives it a good boost. Like humans, the Universe loves being thanked; the more gratitude you give out, the more abundance you will receive, but it has to come from the heart. I am often shown metaphors to help me understand what I am being taught and, in this case, I was shown that gratitude is like pressing the zoom button on a go-kart: when you use that button the go-kart goes extra fast and helps you to reach the destination faster; likewise when you give thanks to the Universe, it helps the wish get to its destination quicker. It is rude to receive a gift and not give thanks to the sender, isn't it? So don't expect abundance if you're going to completely ignore the energy that provides it.

Sometimes we make a wish and it seems it is not answered or, in fact, the complete opposite of the wish comes true. If the wish involves another specific person, it is harder to fulfil because it is dependent on the other's wishes and destiny. Sometimes the wish may not be a part of our own destiny, or it may not be the right time for the wish to come true. For example, I wished many times to be successful in job interviews and to pass my driving test, but it took up to four times in both cases over a few years before my wish came true. That is because the timing was not right and there was a better job opportunity in my future.

Humankind tends to wish for material and physical things when really we should be wishing for internal progress such as to be more authentic, kind, compassionate, forgiving and loving; these wishes are easier to fulfil because they do not need to be manifested in to a physicality and they only involve oneself. My wishes for internal progress have always come true very rapidly, and we will almost always find that when we get the internal right, the external wishes start unfolding more easily, and they are more likely to stay in our lives. If our wishes for materialism and physicality come true whilst we are not working on our internal and spiritual wellbeing, it is very likely that we will be unfulfilled and the material achievements will not last.

The Power of the Right Relationship

Like many relationships, my relationship with my partner was not all sunshine and sparkles; losing my dad and grandad at a young age has had adverse impacts on my life and my ability to trust people. I had a recurring dream from childhood where my mum and twin sister would be walking away from me. I would try to catch up with them but they would get further, and further away until they were black specks in the distance and then they would be gone. I would run around in a panic, looking for them everywhere. This dream changed soon after I met my partner. It was no longer my mum and twin sister walking away from me; it was my partner. This dream always felt very real and it was very upsetting. Often I would wake up and have to look over to check my partner was there. Many times the emotions I felt in the dream such as fear and betrayal were felt for the rest of the day. I taught myself to be very aware of my thoughts on these days so that I would not act on them as if the betrayal had actually happened. When we are reliving an emotion, our brain will react to it as if the event has happened and it will go into protective mode. Protective mode looks different for everyone but for me it looks like defensiveness – getting away from the potential source of hurt before the hurt happens – and this was often manifested as anger and/or isolation. I was essentially reliving the event of losing my dad time and time again. Fortunately, as I have worked on my inner-self and my trust issues, this dream is almost completely gone from my life, and the very few occasions it has returned, I have not had an emotional reaction to it. But in the early stages of my relationship, and for many years prior, I acted out my feelings of fear and betrayal completely unconsciously and, in the midst of that, I hurt the people I loved the most: my mum, my twin sister, my partner and close friends. It was my relationship with my partner that unearthed this awareness and ultimately began the healing.

There were three important things that my partner did that encouraged my self-awareness (unbeknownst to him). Firstly, he accepted me as I am, and that included my grief and fear of abandonment. His complete acceptance of me and all my flaws helped me to accept myself and, in the process, I began to release resistance, and thus became more aware of my inner turmoil. Secondly, he did not enable my grief. Acceptance is not enabling; acceptance is appreciating another as they are without the desire to change them. Enabling is making excuses for a person or allowing their negative behaviour. I clearly remember my partner saying to me that my grief for my dad was not an excuse for my angry outburst. This felt heartless at the time but, on reflection, I understood that by blaming my dad's death, I was not taking responsibility for my actions. Thirdly, my partner taught me the art of forgiveness. I have never heard my partner bring up the past; he simply moves on and lives for the present day. I held resentment and victim mentality following my dad's passing for many years. My relationship taught me the importance of moving forward. I won't give my partner full credit for my inner healing and progress – he planted the seed by being his authentic self and setting an example – but I made the choice to self-reflect, to move forward and to apply what my relationship has taught me to my life. It is important that people do not read this as *My partner healed me.*' That would be a burden for my partner to carry as it may be implying that I would be broken if our relationship ended, and I would be right back to that four-year-old child, lost and fearful. You should never rely on anyone to be your crutch. People can guide you; most people you meet and certainly significant people in your life will teach you lessons, but it is up to you to learn the lesson and to apply the knowledge to your life. This is where we have free will and can choose or change our destiny. Had I not chosen to take action, to continue to behave as the lost child, it is very likely that my relationship would have broken down and my resistance to moving forward would have impacted Dad's ability to connect to me. The experiences I share in this book from here on happened once the healing process began. Dad's connection to me became stronger and evermore magical because I was increasing my energy frequency.

Although my partner would not call himself a spiritual person, he was applying spiritual practice to his daily life far better than I was. My partner finds it easier to be present in the moment than I do; he is forgiving and he loves without condition. Initially I found my partner's ability to love without condition very confusing and, even now, I still have a hard time believing that he can love me without condition.

We were sitting on the sofa sharing a bottle of wine when I asked my partner: *"What do you love about me?"*

I was offended when he didn't immediately rhyme off a list but instead said, *"Everything."*

"Yes, but what exactly," I said.

His reply was, *"I just love you."*

I wasn't satisfied with this and rhymed off all the things I love about him. I spent some time overthinking this the following day: *'I clearly love him more than he loves me,'* I thought. A few months later, I realised the significance of what my partner had said – *"I just love you"* – if my partner does not have a list of things he loves about me, then I do not need to worry about meeting the expectations on the list. How incredibly liberating to know that my partner just loves me. I even began to feel guilty that I had rhymed a list off to him. I considered that if we are doing life right, we are unlikely to be the same person on that list in five years' time anyway because life is about growth and change. If my partner had limited his love for me to the person I was when we first met seven years ago, he could not possibly love me today; I am a completely different person.

I had this newfound freedom I'd never had before. All my life I had acted on what I thought other people's expectations were of me and this was different dependent on who I was with: I was outgoing and bubbly around my friends; reserved and focused around my colleagues; and teenage grumpy around my immediate family. Typically I was daring, active and adventurous around my partner because that was how I perceived him, and that was how I thought he wanted me to be. But now he was giving me permission to be anyone I wanted to be, and of course this raised the question: who am I? This was a challenge in itself. I began peeling back the layers of myself, the choices I had made and the person I aspired to be. I realised the person I aspired to be was not my own aspirations but those of everyone around me. I aspired to be who I thought they wanted me to be and I realised that some of the choices I had made to become this person were harmful to other people. I cringe when a 'Facebook memory' pops up on my newsfeed as I reflect that the words typed on the status were not my own, but for the benefit of the audience I wished to please. It is not easy picking a part ourselves: it is brutal. It has taken me many years to let go of the person I aspired to be. I spent a lot of time and money on that person; I was terrified to let her go.

From a very young age we are asked what we want to be when we grow up. The world tells us we should have a goal in our mind and we should spend time and often money on sculpting ourselves to be just that. In the process of focusing on that end goal of who we wish to be, we lose the essence of what we truly are, because who we truly are is never an end goal: it is our response and our choices in the very moment. *'But my response in the moment depends on what mood I am in.'* Sometimes we say or do some things we do not mean because we are having a bad day or a good day. When you become aware of your true essence within, you become aware of your emotional responses and you tend not to say or do some things that you do not mean because you no longer identify with your emotions. Eventually the façade you put on for the benefit of others becomes exhausting. You may begin to feel depressed, lost, irritated, angry, unfulfilled or emotional for no apparent reason. Some people find a way to unearth this within us, like my partner managed to with his comment; some people experience a crisis like a bereavement or a life changing accident; and, for others, it may be a gradual process with no apparent trigger. Either way, it is an incredibly difficult journey and there is no end. You don't get to the end of the journey and find out who you are; the only antidote is finding peace in not knowing. Some people will be highly offended or confused by this. A gentleman once said to me that he found it terribly sad that I could not say who I am; he found a false sense of power and fulfilment in seemingly knowing who he is but as he ages and the circumstances in his life inevitably change, he will begin to lose elements of who he believes he is and that, for him, will feel incredibly sad. This gentleman has assumed that because I do not know who I am, I am lost, unintelligent or confused so he has already attached a concept to who he believes I am. And there we have it: do not worry if you cannot tell someone who you are, because they will decide who you are anyway.

There is an incredible liberty to not knowing who you are when you can simply accept that fact, because there are no expectations or goal posts: you are free to simply be and you will find that when you are able to simply be without the preconceptions, somehow you have the knowledge to do whatever it is you are supposed to do in that moment. So whilst many people joke that they are 'tied down' in a relationship or 'free' when a relationship ends, this was not the case for me at all. I found my freedom in my relationship. When I type about connecting to your true self within this book, this means connecting to your Soul which has no attachments or form; it simply is as it is in any given moment. When you are connected to your Soul or your Truth within, you will always make choices that are in your best interests and that serve your purpose here on earth, but you have no attachment to expectation or outcome. You don't make a choice because you are this person or that person; you simply make a choice based on what feels right within.

For many years I believed that a strong relationship was two people who become one person. I believed I would be *complete* when I would finally meet my 'soulmate'. However, I have always been a bit of a loner and I always struggled with having to spend more than two days per week with my ex-boyfriends. This was in part why a lot of my previous relationships did not last beyond one year. They would say it was strange that I didn't want to spend any time with them and I agreed. I had just thought I must not love them enough. My partner and I have a lot in common and so I figured it would be easy for us to spend a lot of time together as we enjoy doing the same things. Fortunately, my partner has a hobby that can be time-consuming and most of his friends were single when we first met so they would meet often, which I never discouraged my partner from doing because I enjoyed the time to myself. Many people expect their partners to give up their hobbies and to prioritise their need to spend time with them; they may suggest they are 'too old' to continue with that hobby, they are spending too much money or time on that hobby and this should be invested in their spouse or children. They may feel insecure in the relationship and fear this hobby will take their partner away, or they may find the hobby an unattractive quality. Whilst relationships require compromise, there is no need for anyone to have to cease their hobbies or interests to be in the relationship. To have a hobby is to find joy and purpose in life and hobbies are often respite from the difficulties of a person's job or even home life. Why would you wish to take joy away from the person you claim to love? When a person loves you, they will make time to spend with you and it is perfectly achievable to do so whilst also having a hobby. My partner works very hard. He works six days a week and long hours as we are trying to save to buy our own home. He went many months without prioritising his hobby because he would spend his one day off a week with me. When he told me that he would be spending some of his one day off doing his hobby, I was overjoyed because I knew this would make him happy. Now if my partner was spending his one day off a week doing his hobby every week, I would ask that he would make time for me but I would suggest that he take two days off work per week, not that he would give up his hobby. On this particular day, my partner and I went for a walk for a couple of hours before he went to do his hobby. This was short but it was the most quality time we had had together in a while. This was because on the days we were spending the full day together, I would pick up on my partner's depleted energy; he would present as his usual happy, energetic self but I could feel his inner child was worn down and needed to play. So when he had this day doing his hobby, our short time together was at a higher frequency. We had more meaningful conversations and we laughed more. My point is spending all day every day with your partner does not make the relationship stronger, indeed it may do the opposite. We know that quality is better than quantity; it is far better to spend one joyous day together than five miserable, depleted days together. The strength of a relationship is not two people who become one person: it is two people who remain two people. If two were to become one, then at least one person has to sacrifice themselves. Firstly, many people do not want to sacrifice their uniqueness and freedom, and, secondly, it is a very big burden to expect another person to make you complete. Relationships are not supposed to make us whole: relationships are two already complete people who have individual paths to walk on this earth. Many times the paths will align and many times the paths will detach but the instigator of this path – the one who has the power – is always the self, never the other and it is too much to expect the other to determine your path, or to have the power to make you happy. This is an unachievable expectation that many people believe a romantic relationship will bring them and unless both parties recognise this is a falsehood, the relationship will be unfulfilling and will most likely end. When the path in a relationship detaches, this is perfectly normal and should be expected; very few people grow at exactly the same rate, and very few people experience life exactly the same. So, the real strength of a relationship is when the couple can support, encourage and accept this process and, with patience and love, allow this to unfold as it naturally should without trying to encourage their partner to get on to their path. When we can simply BE in a relationship, instead of trying to control the course of the relationship, what is destined and what is right will unfold as it should. Everyone's journey is their own, and it is no one's place to interfere with another's life and try to change their journey. We can offer advice and guidance, but we should not tell another what they should be doing with their life (unless they are considering threats of harm to themselves or others). In a relationship, the outcome of this is very rarely positive and mostly results in conflict, resentment and infidelity. The saying: 'If you love me, let me go,' is quite literally true. Many people cling on to a person or to a relationship believing that they will be incomplete without it, but we were never incomplete. We were born into this world whole and we will leave this world whole. You will realise that if you let go of your partner; if you allow them to be all that they wish to be and all that they are capable of being, you will see the best in them, and they will see the best in you. In many cases the relationship will flourish and, in many cases, the relationship will end but you are more likely to end on good terms and to have learnt all that you were destined to learn from that relationship. If you were to continue to cling on to this person and relationship, and to limit yourself or the other person, the relationship will inevitably end because it will be one of dishonesty and misery. You should never have to give up or hide anything that brings you joy to make another person happy. If you are in a relationship and the other person's choices are making you unhappy, you have to consider if you want to continue in that relationship. First, I suggest you think about whether the other person's choices are really making you unhappy, or whether your thoughts about the other person's choices are actually the issue. The latter is very different and many people end relationships misunderstanding this and later have regrets.

We can make up some really dramatic stories in our head and completely sabotage an otherwise healthy relationship. Sadly this is often influenced by those around us: people seem to find great satisfaction in analysing other people's relationships. My partner and I have been on the receiving end of this throughout our seven-year relationship. For a short time this was very difficult for me and I would dread social gatherings or avoid particular people who I knew would pry without any consideration for our personal circumstances. Some of the many comments included:

- You STILL aren't living together?
- If you don't ask her to marry you soon, someone else will.

- Any news?
- Any change in the relationship?

One of the most hurtful comments was when we were at a friend's wedding and a gentleman we barely knew commented that if my partner had not asked me to marry him by now, he clearly does not want to be with me. Again, he did not consider our personal circumstances or wishes. We attach an expectation to the rate at which a relationship should be progressing and the majority of us assume that physicality such as owning a home, marriage and having children determine the strength of a relationship, and without these the relationship is unstable. But this is not true. A relationship can have all of this as easily as a person's finances will allow it but, without a foundation of emotional stability, and personal and mutual development, the relationship is weak. As I have highlighted, the strength of a relationship is when a couple can love one another unconditionally as two separate wholes. This unconditional love will manifest as accepting our spouse throughout their individual journey. This may look like a lazy day in your pyjamas without make-up and knowing you are still beautiful to them; encouraging your partner to go on that weekend away with their friends because you know they need it, and without resenting them for it; having the confidence to tell your partner you are scared or sad, or to share your wildest dreams, knowing that no matter how unachievable they may seem right now, your partner will encourage and support your efforts to get there anyway; talking through a problem together instead of arguing about who is right or wrong; realising that your partner has a really great quality and learning to apply that quality to your own life; or recognising that your partner has an unhealthy habit and helping them to overcome this. The real strength of a relationship is unquestionable trust in one another, challenging one another to become more authentic, healthier individuals whilst accepting one another through the process. It is forgiveness, trial and error, selflessness and unconditional love. These are the qualities that make the investment of buying a house into the security of the lifelong home. I have friends who have married, had children and separated in the time my partner and I have been together and so there really is no comparison. It is a tragedy when a healthy, loving relationship breaks down because the influence of those around them has convinced them it is not how it should be. I am not saying that these physicalities are not important in a relationship; they can represent commitment and maturity. If living together, marriage, children, etc. is something you want in your relationship, you should be able to have open conversations about this with your partner. You should talk about dreams and plans for the future that will involve this and you will be proactive in doing all that you can to achieve these goals. If your long-term partner is clearly avoiding these conversations or avoiding opportunities to progress in these areas, you may want to consider going your separate ways.

In any case, in order for the external progress to be a success, the couple must at least have some awareness of their own internal being. We carry so much emotional baggage with us throughout our lives. As children we learn to bury our fears, sadness and anger because the adults in our lives tell us to do just that. Adults try to protect children by not telling them what's going on, for example, and so the child may be scared to ask (bury that fear away), or when the child does ask, they are berated or dismissed (bury that sadness away). If the child is frustrated and lashes out, they are chastised (bury that anger away). These emotions don't just disappear; they are stored in our subconscious and are reflected in our behaviour. They take us away from our innocence and the pureness we are all born with. We avoid dealing with these buried emotions by keeping ourselves busy. Some people can't stand their own company because they begin to feel scared, worried or sad. When we don't recognise that these emotions are coming from within, we start to blame them on our external environment and particularly our partner because they are typically the most familiar person in our life. We become angry, sad and blameful when our partner no longer makes us feel that excited, fuzzy feeling inside; we believe there must be something wrong with the relationship, or something must be missing. This often results in the relationship ending, or results in infidelity, because the individual wants to find the excited, fuzzy feeling again but until they look within, their relationships will keep failing. I had never recognised myself as the jealous type but when I met my partner and fell in love, I struggled to see him getting on with other females and we would argue. I eventually realised this was a reflection of my childhood grief and fear of losing another man I loved, and had nothing to do with my partner. My relationship encouraged me to recognise this buried emotion, release it and move forward. Many people blame their relationship for making them feel insecure, when actually the relationship is not responsible for this at all. It was already within but it lay dormant until the opportunity arose for it to come forward. This is how relationships can encourage spiritual and personal development because they unearth undesirable emotions and give us the opportunity to recognise, release and heal. When you are in conflict with your partner, listen to what is being said: often it is so petty it is humorous. If you can be aware of your internal being, you can recognise the emotion behind the conflict: jealousy, anger, fear, an inner child demanding love and attention. Are you really upset that your partner is watching football instead of going for a walk with you? Or is this your inner child demanding attention from an absent father? Notice how you may overreact to a minor circumstance and feel silly for it later, but you're too stubborn to take ownership and apologise to your partner, so they get the silent treatment anyway. Try to allow yourself the time to reflect on why you reacted the way you did. Whatever the emotion, there is always a root cause. A relationship cannot withstand external progress without internal progress. It is more helpful if both partners can be internally aware but, if at least one partner can practise internal awareness, this can unearth that awareness in the other and the relationship can be salvaged if both partners wish it to be. Indeed, in the early stages of my relationship, I was very unaware and my partner unearthed the internal awareness and progress in me. Whilst my relationship encouraged the early stages of my internal realisation, what would happen next in my life influenced my most profound awakening.

Chapter 5

Can I Call Him Daddy?

I remember the day my mum told us she had a new partner. I was around seven years old and I asked her if I could call him daddy. I could see that she was taken aback, and so even though she quickly composed herself and explained that I could if I wanted to, I knew she was not comfortable with this. My step-dad absolutely adored my twin sister and me; he would never have said it, but it was clear we were his favourites. He was always scooping us up on to his knee and pulling our hair bobbles out to get our attention; we could do no wrong in his eyes. My older sisters struggled with the concept of a 'new dad' so he wasn't exactly welcomed with open arms and his attempts to put boundaries in place often went ignored. However, he was very respectful of my dad and I don't believe he ever wished to replace him.

I remember the first time I learnt to trust my step-dad. I was around eight years old and I had been to the swimming baths with a school friend. I had chlorine in my eye and this was very painful for me. I spent the rest of the day lying on the sofa feeling sorry for myself. My step-dad comforted me and told me it would be better in the morning, but I was in so much pain I didn't believe it could ever get better. The next morning I woke up and I was indeed better. I remember my disbelief and joy. I told my step-dad I was better and he scooped me up onto his knee and said, *"I told you."* I trusted him from that very moment.

There were many times when I would cry about petty arguments with my sisters and my step-dad would comfort me. I've lost count of the times he would drive me to job interviews and comfort me when I didn't get the offer; he was always convinced that I was going to get the job, and, when I didn't, he would make a degrading comment about the panel and state that there was something wrong with them. He would remind me not to study too hard but he would actively look out for articles that would help me with my university studies.

My step-dad was incredibly supportive but there was one thing he used to do that was absolutely awful: he used to make the worst pasta bake, and for many years my siblings and I were too polite to tell him that we did not like it, so we would pretend to eat it and secretly put it under the table or in the bin. He figured this out, or Mum told him after a few years, because he stopped making it. There are many things I miss about my step-dad but his pasta bake is not one of them.

It was Friday 17th March 2017 and my first day off work in six days. My days off were pretty predictable at my twenty-six years of age; run, bath, put on dressing gown and read my book. However, this day would be my first run of the week. Normally I would have been out running at least three times by now but I had been asked to work overtime. I was working at my twin sister's cafe at this time and it was peak season which meant that I could be on my feet for up to nine hours each day, so my feet were sore and I would just go to bed after my shift. I remember I was so looking forward to getting out on this run. As I was lacing up my shoes, I heard my step-dad call my name. I popped my head around the door; he was sitting in his chair as per usual and he asked if I would make him a cup of tea. I remember thinking it strange that he asked me as he had never asked me to make him anything in the whole twenty years he had been 'Dad'. I found it even stranger when I noticed that he had actually started making the cup of tea himself, but for some reason couldn't finish making it. Nevertheless, I tutted under my breath at the half a cup of sugar he had put in there, before handing him his tea and heading out on my run. My step-dad would always ask how far I had run and sometimes he would time me which always annoyed me. I would say to him, *"I'm not competing with myself,"* and I would roll my eyes as he laughed, fully aware that he was tormenting me. I didn't much notice that he didn't comment on my running that day.

I was about twenty minutes into my book when I overheard my step-dad walking up the stairs. I noted that he seemed to be struggling with his breathing but he was a heavy smoker and so he often struggled walking up the stairs. Still, I quickly thought up an excuse to go on to the landing and check he was OK. As I put my book down I heard my step-dad fall. I rushed to him but he asked that I leave him for a moment. He said he would get himself back up. I ran downstairs to find the inhaler the doctor had prescribed him just days earlier; something felt very wrong and I was panicking. Whilst I mustn't have been searching for more than ten to fifteen seconds, it felt like a lifetime, rummaging through his cluttered corner by his chair trying to find his inhaler. By the time I got back to him, my step-dad had gone into cardiac arrest but I did not realise this at the time. I just knew something wasn't right. I told him I was ringing for an ambulance. My step-dad was at least six feet tall, and of stocky build; I was seven and a half stone and five feet two. There was no way I could roll him over to perform CPR, and so I knocked for my neighbours and I hid in the living room whilst they tried to save his life. My last memory is standing in my front garden in my dressing gown, shouting at the First Responder because I felt she was taking too long to park the ambulance.

I felt a lot of shame after my step-dad's death; I felt that if I had not panicked or if I had only found the strength to roll him over and to start the CPR a moment sooner, then he would have lived. I had read that the last sense people lose when they pass away is their hearing, and so I had an awful fear that he may have heard me panicking and this may have made him feel frightened. I felt terribly guilty that I had not stayed with him, reassuring him when my neighbours were trying to save his life, and I was convinced my family also believed that I was partly responsible for his death.

A few nights after my step-dad passed away, I dreamt that Mum and I were visiting him in hospital. He was sitting upright in the hospital bed and he looked bright. I told him I was worried that he could hear me panicking; he laughed and told me that he could. I could not understand why he found this funny as I did not find it funny at all, and I was not in the least bit reassured when he clarified that he had indeed heard me panicking. For a long while after this dream, I fantasised that this was the outcome; even if he had passed away in the hospital bed, at least we would have had the chance to say goodbye.

My step-dad's passing changed me; I could never go back to the person I was before. Where I was once someone who couldn't sleep if there was a little light shining through the crack in the door, I became scared of the dark and for almost a year I slept with my bedroom lamp on when my partner wasn't staying with me. I developed incredibly low self-esteem and I would often look in the mirror and cry. For almost a year I was convinced I was dying. I would lie in bed and plan my own funeral. I would consider who would be good enough to take care of my partner so that he would not grieve for me forever. Whenever I had to walk past the top of the stairs, I would walk really fast so as to get away from it before I could be reminded of the day I could not save my step-dad's life.

When I was eventually told by my General Practitioner (GP) that I may be suffering with a form of Post-Traumatic Stress

Disorder (PTSD), I began researching it and I was able to rationalise my thoughts and feelings. I have a degree in counselling so I am somewhat familiar with the fundamentals of Cognitive Behavioural Therapy and other counselling theories which helped me immensely during this time. I was able to consider the PTSD as separate from who I am, and so when the self-loathing and fear arose, I acknowledged it and I considered that if I were to be kind to it, it would either leave, or it would eventually flourish into something beautiful and then I wouldn't mind it hanging around. So whenever I felt bad when I looked in the mirror or scared when I was in the dark, I would stop and imagine the energy as a grizzly goblin and I would shower it with love and then I would imagine it turning in to a cute little goblin that just wanted to be acknowledged and loved. This worked incredibly well for me, and I was able to move forward from my trauma in a matter of months without any medication or counselling. I realise now that I could have avoided that whole year of sadness and fear by acknowledging my sadness and fears straight away. We all feel guilty, sad, angry and scared sometimes, especially when we experience a trauma but we must not try to run away from those emotions. We must not say, *"I should not be feeling this way; it is wrong."* These emotions are a very important part of our human experience, spiritual development and Soul purpose. The sooner we acknowledge them, and do not label them as wrong but rather accept them, the sooner we will heal and learn the lesson we are destined to learn. I could never be the same person with this newfound knowledge, as I found an inner strength and a resilience that I had never known before. Most wonderfully, I went from being terrified of death to having no fear of death at all.

My Guiding Light

My step-dad's death would trigger an intense spiritual awakening, and to this day, he visits me regularly in my dreams.

When I first saw my step-dad in my dreams, I would cry and cry and cry and he would just hold me. Often within those dreams he delivers a message, but I rarely remember the words that are exchanged between us. I believe I am reminded of the messages from my step-dad when they become relevant in my daily life. For example, I often have '*aha*' moments or I realise I just know something very wise, but I do not know how I know it.

I know that my step-dad was on a journey within the first year of his passing as I saw a great deal of progress in each visitation. My step-dad did not transition straight away as is often the case with people who pass away suddenly. I know this because he showed me in my dreams that he was working his way through levels and that there was other Spirit with him, either helping him, or transitioning themselves.

My step-dad had a significant development around one year after passing away and this is when he would go to the Heaven level. In this dream my mum was with me, we were in what might have been a beautiful green park, and we were sitting on a bench waiting to say goodbye to my step-dad. My mum was very nervous and she was constantly looking out for him. I think at one point she was worried that he was not going to come. My step-dad appeared with a huge grin on his face saying *"Hello, my lovelies"* whilst he opened his arms for an embrace. In this dream he taught me that everyone is given the opportunity to say goodbye to their loved ones but not everyone remembers it. I noticed then that there were other benches with people waiting to say goodbye to their loved ones – these were people who passed away suddenly – and on the benches sat the loved ones who did not get the opportunity to say goodbye to the Spirit person whilst they were on this earth. I had expected that this would be the last visit I would have from my step-dad since he had now gone to Heaven, but thankfully it was not.

After this dream, I stopped crying when I saw my step-dad in my dreams as I developed an understanding that this was an opportunity to spend time with him and so I must make the most of it. When I am dreaming of my step-dad, we are never in the same environment and often he will have an item that stands out to me and helps me to remember the dream. For example, once he wore a green cast on his ankle as though it was broken; coincidently my sister-in-law broke her ankle a few days after I had this dream. Once I was waiting for him in a church and we walked around the church for what felt like an eternity; he taught me a great deal during this visit. Another time he picked me up in an old-fashioned white car. My step-dad loved cars; I'm not an expert but I Googled the make of this car and it looked like a Volvo 144, which was a popular car in the 1950s when my step-dad would have been in his youth. We have met in cafes, shops, and at my mum's house. It has been a lot easier for me to move forward from my step-dad's passing because he visits me so regularly in my dreams.

In the past, if I was going through a stressful time, my body would react by getting a urinary tract infection (UTI). There was a period of a few years post my step-dad's passing that I would get UTIs quite regularly. Anyone who has experienced this will know how uncomfortable and often painful this infection can be. I had developed a UTI at the beginning of the week, and I had to phone in to work sick. This really disgruntled me as I had only been in this job four months and I didn't want a black mark next to my name. More so, I couldn't afford to take time off. I spent the day trying to flush it out with fluids so that I wouldn't have to phone in to work sick for a second day. I got myself back in to bed mid-afternoon, hoping I may be able to have some rest between my ten minute toilet trips. Thankfully, I was able to fall asleep. In my dream, I met my step-dad at a hospital; he was walking with me to see a specific lady who could help me to feel better. He was talking to me about this lady but I cannot remember what he said. Though I do remember him telling me that I must take the next day off work to rest. He said: *"If they can manage without you today, they can manage without you tomorrow."* I woke up feeling much better, though I still had a slightly raised temperature and nausea so I followed my step-dad's advice to take another day off work. Had I not had this dream, I would have definitely gone in to work as I needed the money at that time and I couldn't afford to miss more than one day's pay, but I wasn't about to ignore my step-dad's advice (I've heard stories of people who ignored a spiritual dream and ended up having an accident or a traumatic experience that could have been avoided had they only listened to the dream). I went in to work on the Wednesday and spoke to a colleague about my annoyance that I was going to miss two days' pay due to sickness. She smiled at me and said, *"Don't you know, we get paid for sick days?"* Now I was really thankful I followed my step-dad's advice. Not only was it a huge relief that I was not going to be short of money at the end of the month, but I was returning to work in much better health than I would have had I returned to work the day prior.

My step-dad is really having a blast in the spirit world. He has shown me that he continues to attend family gatherings and, in my next dream, he was even at my best friend's wedding. My step-dad was very fond of one of my oldest friends, Clo, and she was fond of him too. We have been friends since we were at least four years old, and when she would come to visit, she would jump on his knee and make a big fuss of him, which he loved. He attended her sister's wedding but he had passed away four years prior to Clo's wedding. Due to Covid-19 restrictions, it was a very quiet and intimate wedding. My twin sister and I were able to attend but numbers didn't reach to external family and friends and so, as it turns out, he wouldn't have been able to go anyway. However, one of the many bonuses to being in spirit form is that you can be wherever you want to be at any time you wish to be. I was with my twin sister in this dream when my step-dad appeared; he was standing waiting for me as always. I looked to my sister and told her our step-dad was there but she could not see him. I said again: *"Look, he is right there. Can't you see him?"* Still she couldn't see him and so I threw my hands in the air and told her that he was waiting for me and I would be back later. My step-dad and I embraced one another in a hug. I noted that he smelt very strongly of red wine and he was wearing a suit. He began walking and I was trying to keep up with him. Although I didn't feel rushed, I knew that he was walking with purpose and he had to get me somewhere. As we walked, we laughed and smiled and thoroughly enjoyed one another's company. All the while, I couldn't stop thinking about the fact that he smelt of red wine. *'Why would anyone need to drink red wine in Heaven?'* I kept thinking. As I was thinking this, Spirit was nudging me to ask my step-dad about the red wine but instead I asked: *"Why are you wearing a suit?"* My step-dad replied, *"I got it for The Roundthorn."* I could feel myself coming out of this dream and so I was trying desperately to stay because I had so many more questions I wished to ask him. Unfortunately, I couldn't keep myself there any longer and I woke up.

There are a few lessons my step-dad was teaching me in this dream. Clo's wedding was at Roundthorn Country House and so it was immediately clear to me that my step-dad was showing me that he was at the wedding celebrating with us. This is also why he was wearing a suit and smelt of red wine; my step-dad thoroughly enjoyed red wine and he would have been drinking this at any occasion. My step-dad was also showing me that he can indeed still drink red wine in Heaven because it is something that brings him joy, and we can continue to enjoy earthly pleasures in Heaven if we are still attached to them. The strong smell of red wine was also a factor to help me remember the experience and to highlight that my senses are opening up at a deeper level. My step-dad was keen to get me to wherever it was we needed to be. There were many things going on in my life at that time and I already knew that I was going through another spiritual transition. I believe my step-dad's 'walk with purpose' was him guiding me into this new spiritual journey.

The transition into this new spiritual journey was not easy. I was feeling lost and confused for a few months and my job was becoming increasingly challenging. I was seeing the impact of Covid-19 on people's mental health first-hand; almost every family I was allocated was experiencing a mental health crisis. Mental health services were over stretched and people were not getting the support they needed fast enough. I work in Children's Services, I am not a trained mental health professional and so as much as I wanted to help these families, I did not have the professional skills they needed to help them to get better; there were many days when I felt overwhelmed and helpless. On a Saturday evening, I was tossing and turning in bed unable to sleep; it was incredibly windy outside and every so often the wind would rattle by door knocker so this was keeping me awake, and of course I used this time to worry about work - *why do anxieties arise when we are in bed and should be asleep?* Eventually, I closed my eyes and I was transported to an old train station. I was running uncontrollably down some steps, I could see that I was about to bump into a man and I couldn't stop myself. I fell into his chest but luckily he was strong enough not to tumble over. I looked up to this man and I realised it was my step-dad. I looked straight in to his blue/grey eyes and I burst in to tears. My step-dad pulled me in for a warm embrace and chuckled as he said *"What are you crying for?"* This was a recent visit so by this point, I was not usually crying when I was spending time with my step-dad in my dreams, but I was so tired and I was so relieved to see him that I was overcome with emotion. I said to my step-dad *"I am finding my job very hard"*. As I was saying this I noticed that my step-dad had a brown suitcase next to him. I wanted to have more time with my step-dad but I could feel him fading away, before I knew it I was back in my bedroom and I was still crying.

Ten days after this dream, I was offered a new job. The train station and the suitcase of course, signified that my time in this job was coming to an end. My step-dad was reassuring me that this challenging time would soon be over, and I was about to embark on a new journey in a new job role. This was a lovely message from my step-dad, but I am most thankful that in that moment when life felt so hard, I was allowed to experience the loving embrace from my step-dad. I know many people who have a loved one in the spirit world, would give anything for such an experience.

I am very blessed that I have these experiences with my step-dad; they are no less real to me than my day-to-day life is – more so I am always very aware in my dreams that I am spending time with my step-dad's Spirit. It's not like I think he is alive as I knew him to be in human form; in fact, I am so aware that my step-dad is not alive in human form that I always remind myself during the dream to make the most of every moment because I know it is temporary. I do worry that one day these visits may stop or may become less frequent; my step-dad visits me in my dreams so regularly that I have not had to live life without seeing him, touching him or hearing his voice, like my mum and siblings have.

I think of my step-dad as my Guiding Light because he has taught me so much since his passing. He has helped me to understand that I was supposed to be with him when he went into cardiac arrest because this enabled us to have a special connection, and that this was an event destined to encourage my spiritual development.

I Thought I was Dying

As already mentioned, following my step-dad's death, I became terrified that I was going to die. I had never really thought about death before and so I didn't realise how scared I was of it. When we go through a trauma that affects our mental health, often the body gets sick too. I was experiencing extreme fatigue, nausea, dizziness and my mood was erratic. *'I must have cancer,'* I thought. This fear was keeping me awake at night. One morning I woke up, and decided to relax in bed before rising; I'm not sure if I fell back to sleep or went into a vision, but within this I went down stairs and saw my step-dad in the kitchen. As I walked over to him he said, *"Come here love,"* and, as always, embraced me with a hug. I asked him if I was dead and he replied, *"Yes love."* And then I watched him walk away with me. When I awoke, I had knowledge that a part of me had died and left with my step-dad and that this was necessary for my spiritual awakening. So when I was convinced I was dying, I was not wrong. Somewhere inside of me, I knew I was going through a huge transition which would result in the death of an aspect of my former self. I have since read that the physical symptoms I was experiencing can be a sign of an awakening, as our DNA is changing and our bodies can be exhausted due to the internal energy shift.

This visitation from my step-dad was the beginning of me completely releasing my fear of death. We are constantly dying. The infant body was born and died; the childhood body was born and died; the adolescent body was born and died; the adulthood body was born and died – and we go through this cycle until we get to our senior physical body. This is the greatest transition because we are not reborn as physical form. So we have been dying ever since we were born. In some cases, a part of our identity dies but we are still in the same body cycle and this can be very challenging for the individual going through the internal transition. They may have physical and emotional symptoms due to the change in energy and this can be worrying, as it was for me. They may lose friends and no longer enjoy activities they used to enjoy. During an internal transition, we are purging energies that no longer serve our highest good so this can make us feel very low for a while. You must always seek medical advice when you are experiencing any change in your body or mood. I saw my GP during this transition.

My perception of death has completely changed partly because of what my step-dad has been teaching me since his passing and more so because I know without a shadow of a doubt that there is life after death of the human form. This afterlife, which I will call Heaven is beautiful and safe and nobody gets forgotten or left behind. Whilst I still feel sad when I hear of people passing away, it is mostly for the people who are here on earth for I know the pain they will carry, especially if it is an unexpected passing or the passing of a child or a young person. A friend of mine, who I will call Rose, passed away very unexpectedly. I was very sad when I was told but, again, mostly for her loved ones here on earth. I know that when we pass over we are beginning a beautiful new journey: loved ones in Spirit greet us like we do a newborn baby on earth, with pure love and acceptance. They even prepare and get excited for our arrival. We continue our transition of death and rebirth in the afterlife because we are constantly learning and developing. The ultimate goal for every Soul is to get back to their eternity with God, where we have no identification with form whatsoever. This is really what or who we are. Some people will need to go through a purging before making the full transition to the afterlife and some Spirit may even choose to stay earthbound for a while. This is a part of their journey, just like we have to go through challenging times on earth, but they are always protected and they always find their way to the light.

My friend, Rose, visited me in a dream seven months after she passed away. She was dressed in a ridiculous Halloween costume which was fitting because it was October, but also strange because she hated fancy dress. Spirit may wear something a bit 'out there' to help us remember the visitation and so that the brain doesn't simply interpret it as a memory. Rose told me that she was not ready to pass over when she did, and she was still not ready to pass over. She showed me that she was happily working as a waitress and she joked around with me like she always did here on earth. Rose loved to work; it was a big part of her identity when she was in human form, and so until she was ready to cross over and go to Heaven, God would allow her to have some of that normality and whatever else she needed to feel safe. Rose's passing was very sudden and so she needed help to transition with ease. She needed time to let go of her human attachments like her job as a waitress. This highlights just how much God loves us; when my friend is ready, she will be guided to the light and God will be overjoyed to welcome her home.

People who pass away like to be at their own funeral or their 'send-off'. If you listen to your feelings, you would be able to feel them as they do approach each and every single person at their funeral. I often feel drained after a funeral especially if it is someone very close to me, and so I try to nap late-afternoon or early-evening to recuperate. It was the eve following the funeral of a relative whom I will call Winnie, and I felt exhausted so I took myself to my bedroom for a rest. As I lay in bed and closed my eyes, I saw Winnie sitting on a train dressed smartly with a hat on and she was reading a newspaper. I was looking at Winnie inside the train but I could also see the outside of the train at the same time; I watched as the train lifted off the ground and up into the sky. Winnie had waited to attend her funeral and was now embarking on her journey home to Heaven. Winnie always enjoyed reading the newspaper, so this part made sense to me however, I had only ever seen Winnie wear a hat once before at a family wedding, so I was confused as to why she had a hat on. Then it dawned on me: Winnie wore hats for occasions. Of course she would wear a hat to her own funeral. I asked Winnie to send me a white feather to confirm my vision was really her. An hour or so later, I drove to my partner's house and, as I stepped out of the car, a bright white feather landed at my feet.

I know many people will argue that my experiences are coincidences or even the result of my mind attracting the experiences; I have battled with doubting myself for many years. When I first started receiving signs, visions and dreams, I would get so excited I would want to tell the world about them. I would tell my nearest and dearest and often they would offer another explanation or not say anything at all and I knew that they did not believe me. This was very disheartening and, as a result, I had dismissed a lot of what I was shown when I was younger. However, I have come a long way in recent years; I can appreciate now that my experiences with God and Spirit and all that it is teaching me has brought me a great deal of peace. It has helped me to overcome anxiety, fear of rejection, fear of death. It has taught me the importance of forgiveness and self-love and so much more. I do not carry the burdens or worries that many of my friends, colleagues and family have. I have a sense that I am always guided and protected and this gives me a strength that many people do not have.

I have chosen not to share many of the experiences I share in this book with the people in my life. Indeed, Spirit has discouraged me from sharing my experiences with my family and friends because they know how upsetting it is for me when I am dismissed or mocked. Spirit have reassured me that people who do not want to know about the Spirit world will not buy my book, but also that I must not live my life in fear of what other people think, for that is not a life lived at all.

Chapter 6

Reiki

Reiki has had a significant impact on enhancing my self-awareness and my spiritual development. I had considered reiki for a few years when, one day in January 2020, I eventually decided to Google my local reiki practitioners. The most local was not available after five p.m. or weekends which was no good for me. So then I found Nicki who was a forty-minute drive away but could see me evenings and weekends. I hadn't expected to be attending reiki regularly so I didn't mind the drive. However, my experiences of reiki with Nicki have been so magical and uplifting that I have continued to see her once a month for over two years. I don't believe it is a coincidence that my ability to sense and communicate with Spirit has hugely improved since I started receiving reiki healing. Indeed Spirit has since shown me that meeting Nicki is a part of my destiny.

I was very nervous to attend my first ever reiki healing but as soon as Nicki opened the door, her peaceful presence showered over me and I was instantly put at ease. She told me I may see colours or feel sensations as she was healing areas of my body but I hadn't expected I would, especially as it was my first time. However, early into the session my mind's eye opened up and I saw my step-dad sitting in the corner of the room. He said to me, *"I will sit right here, just like I always did at the dentist."* I was terrified of the dentist as a child and my step-dad used to sit in the appointments with me up until I was fourteen years old. As the session continued, I felt all of the healing which was a strange but amazing experience; Nicki was not physically touching me but I could feel every area of my body that she was working on at each time. Nicki gave me feedback at the end of the session, sharing what she had experienced when doing the healing (it is important to note, that Nicki knew nothing about my life). I had no intention of sharing what I had experienced with my step-dad as I still had reservations about how real these visitations were, but then she said: *"I felt a male energy on this side of the room."* She pointed to my right which was where I had seen my step-dad sitting. This was the verification that I needed and so I shared my experience of my step-dad. In that moment, Nicki and I both received loving energy feels from Spirit, thanking us for acknowledging my step-dad's presence.

I continued to experience beautiful visions and feelings during reiki and in between reiki sessions, but Dad had not been a part of this until around six months in. I was driving to my reiki appointment when suddenly I felt Dad's loving presence with me; I acknowledged him and continued to feel him as I walked into the therapy room. Nicki and I always begin the session with a brief catch up. As we were chatting, Nicki suddenly became overwhelmed with emotion and apologised, stating she did not know what had come over her. I suspected that my dad's energy had something to do with it but I did not share this with Nicki. As the healing began, Nicki gently laid her hands over my head; my mind's eye opened up and I saw my dad's hands in place of Nicki's; again, I did not share this with Nicki at that time. A moment passed and Nicki expressed that she must share that she was feeling a very loving male energy with her. She could see his hands in place of hers and again she was overcome with emotion stating that this male's love for me was incredibly strong. This was my verification, and so I told Nicki this male energy was my dad and that he had been in the car travelling to this session with me. Sometimes we question why Spirit appear when they do and we can drive ourselves crazy trying to figure out the meaning behind it. Often there isn't a great meaning; they just want to show their loved ones that they are around them. The best thing we can do is acknowledge them and accept their love.

It was during reiki that I was allowed to see my Guardian Angel. Guardian Angels do not have any attachment to a body or a sex. However, my Guardian Angel chose to appear as a male wearing a red velvet suit, with gold leaf patterns, and shoulder-length blond hair; there were no wings or a halo, but he did appear very royal. As my communication is predominantly *feel*, I felt this person gave an Angelic presence and so I knew it was an Angel – I just didn't realise it was my Guardian Angel initially. He stood at the bottom of the therapy bed and slowly walked to my head where Nicki was standing. After the healing, I told Nicki of my experience and shared that I knew this was a significant Angel but I didn't know of any Archangels who wore red. As Nicki and I pondered on this, it was as if I was hit by a bolt of lightning. I shot up from where I was lying on the bed to a seated position and I called out, *"It was my Guardian Angel."* I have never had a knowing as strong as I did in that moment. I knew without a shadow of a doubt that I had just seen my Guardian Angel. I thanked Nicki profusely for intertwining her incredible energy with mine to allow me to see my Guardian Angel.

Lorna Byrne states that we can all see our Guardian Angel if only we ask, and if only we believe. I believe many people attach a condition to their belief of their Guardian Angel: *'I will believe it when I see it.'* This puts us at a very low frequency and makes it difficult for our Guardian Angel, who is at a very high frequency, to manifest a form that we can see with the human eye. I had learnt to appreciate feeling and not seeing. I loved my Guardian Angel for all that he was doing to help me even without seeing him. So I believe that my unconditional belief in my Guardian Angel intertwined with mine and Nicki's high frequency energy, allowed my Guardian Angel to manifest a physical form for my benefit in that moment. Whilst I am very grateful for this experience, I am now spiritually aware enough to appreciate my Guardian Angel as simply energy without any form, but it is wonderful to have an image in my mind to refer back to.

My experiences during reiki are so magical, I could write reams on them. However, they may not make much sense to you; they are tailored to meet my individuality and serve my growth. Spirit will talk to us in terms we understand. They will show us words or visions that we are able to relate to. Spirit could deliver the same message to many people in many different ways; they will tailor it to the individual's perceptions, beliefs and experiences. Many people will not have visions or *feels* during reiki but will experience the benefits of a clear mind after a healing session which allows more space for divinely inspired ideas, or they may find that a situation that had occupied so much of their energy, no longer feels so significant. They may just feel better but can't put their finger on what the difference is. We are all made up of energy, and energy can become stagnant. Reiki helps the energy to flow smoothly again so it is very likely that anyone who receives reiki healing will feel at least a little lighter, unless they are completely unaware of their body – in which case I don't expect they would even seek out reiki healing.

We all have hobbies, activities or practices that we feel called to in our life; we must remember that our journey on earth is unique to us. I do recommend reiki to all my friends and family because it continues to have such a profound impact on my spiritual journey. However, not everyone will find that reiki benefits their life and may choose another method of healing. What is necessary to all of humankind is the importance of growth, and in order to grow, we must heal; we must find a method that suits us and enables us to get closer to our Soul, our Truth within.

Healing

We all carry our grief differently; my dad's death has impacted me, my mum and my five siblings very differently. Whilst writing this book, I have developed an understanding that my dad's death has taught all of my family something that is necessary for our Souls' development. When I understood this my thoughts went something like this: *'Whoa, my dad literally sacrificed himself to help our development.'* Spirit don't see it like that. In fact life on earth is a lot more challenging than life in the afterlife so it is those who have stuck it out here the longest who are the real warriors. Dad learnt what he was supposed to whilst he was here, and our family was a part of that. It is always more painful for the grieving people left here on earth, and my family agreed to experience the grief to support Dad's journey; so the sacrifice is equal both ways. The bereavement of my dad has taught me a lot. I believe it has made me a better person and has increased my understanding of this life and the afterlife. Had I not lost my dad, I probably wouldn't have explored spirituality and the afterlife as much as I have, and then I wouldn't have the connection to my spiritual self, which gives me such peace, courage and self-awareness. Would I go back and wave a magic wand so that my dad or step-dad could have lived longer on this earth? No, absolutely not, and I know they wouldn't want that either but I haven't always felt this way.

For many years I felt that Dad's death should not have happened. I felt he was catastrophically failed by our local medical practice; he went to the GP multiple times with symptoms but he was always sent away. It was my mum who argued with the GP that my dad was not well and he must be referred for further examination. I felt that had they listened to my dad sooner, he would have been cured or, at the very least, given more time on earth with his family. I was bitter and angry and often I unconsciously took this out on my nearest and dearest, causing a lot of pain for them and a lot of guilt for myself. You can imagine how angry I was then, when my step-dad went to the GP on Monday feeling unwell, was sent home almost immediately, and then passed away on the Friday. I even contacted a Lawyer, who said I may have a case, but I was gently reminded by a relative that my family were grieving too, and this may only prolong the pain.

We always want to have someone to blame, especially in situations where we have been caused pain. Instead of looking internally, we immediately look for the externals at fault. Some people believe justice will bring them peace, but nothing external will bring peace: we must go within and focus on healing ourselves. *What is the lesson this experience is trying to teach me?* In instances of murder, exploitation and other despicable criminal acts, people must serve their time and they do – even if they don't on this earth, they do in the afterlife. They feel the pain they caused this person and their loved ones for what may feel like an eternity, until they have learnt compassion and sorrow for their act. However, those who have been wronged often carry anger and pain, and they are unable to forgive, causing themselves even more suffering. If they don't release these low frequency emotions in this lifetime, they must in the afterlife. That is not to say it is not OK to feel heartache for the loss of a loved one; that comes from a place of love and is instantly re-leased when we return home and see our love ones again. Anger, blame and non-forgiveness are much lower frequencies and a lot of work must be done to release these as they are so far re-moved from our Truth, our Soul. People who carry these emo-tions into the afterlife get lots of support from Spirit who helps them to heal and guides them back to their Truth.

During a meditation, Spirit showed me 'The Room of For-giveness', it was a bright white room with different shades of pink and green. I could see the whole room and I knew I was in the centre of it however I couldn't see myself, at least not how I know myself to be with a physical form. It was like I was me in the centre of this room, but I was also me surrounding the room, observing myself. Whilst I was taking in my surroundings, Spirit told me that this was The Room of Forgiveness, so I instantly began thinking of all the people I thought I needed to forgive, and then Spirit stopped me and told me that I was not to think of forgiving anyone else, but I was to go within and to focus on forgiving myself. I was confused by this and even a little of-fended, and this brought me out of the vision. My visions are only a small part of my learning, I will often experience infor-mation downloads days, weeks and sometimes even months af-ter the vision which helps me to understand the experience.

I was surprised that I reacted the way I did in this vision as I thought I had a good understanding of the importance of self-love however, my reaction to what Spirit had said to me was ignorant and highlighted areas of personal development that I thought I had met but clearly I have not. Though, I knew the significance of this vision - that I could not forgive anyone until I learnt to forgive myself, that I must take responsibility and that we are all connected; healing always starts from within, and whether we like it or not, we are entirely responsible for our own emotions. I know that we all go to The Room of Forgiveness when we pass over to the Spirit world, and I'm certain there are other rooms we also have to go to, to help us to remember our Truth. Spirit has told me there is a room called 'Gods Classroom' but they did not show me this room. I hope they take me there whilst I am here on earth, perhaps I could then share the experience with others.

Due to the nature of my job, I see many clients with a victim mentality that rant and rave about all the awful things someone has done to them. They so often say: *"S/he is the reason I'm like this. S/he messed me up."* And I always say to them: *"You may not be responsible for their actions, but you are entirely responsible for how you respond to them."* The saying, *'You are not responsible for other people's feelings'* is incredibly profound and incredibly liberating when we can really grasp what this means. If you are responsible for your own feelings, that means the other is also responsible for their own feelings. This realisation changed my life.

I am what some people might call 'a people pleaser.' I love any opportunity to help people; it gives me purpose knowing that I am making someone's day a little better. However, this hasn't always been well reciprocated by others, especially where Spirit have nudged me to share a message that the other wasn't ready to hear. When someone has been offended by my words or action, I have felt incredibly guilty. I would over-analyse it for weeks and I would feel physically sick at the thought of causing another's pain or sadness. Some days this would feel unbearable and I would not want to get out of bed. Though I have not always felt such guilt. I am not a saint, far from it, and there have been times in my past when I was far less conscious, where I have done or said something to deliberately hurt another, as a type of revenge when they have hurt my feelings. In this case, we can take some responsibility for another's emotions because we have actively sought to hurt them. Still, the other can choose to accept your deliberate attempt to hurt them and let it be a success, or they can choose to be aware of how it made them feel, let it go, and continue with their life unaffected by your actions.

I was feeling very low about a situation where I had unintentionally hurt another's feelings. I was berating myself, and I asked that Spirit would let me take my words back, when they enveloped me in a warm embrace and reassured me that my words were never said out of malice: they were said from a place of love. Spirit reminded me that I am a good, kind person and I would never wish to harm any being. They reassured me that this person has chosen to take offence and that is their own doing, not mine. This brought me a great deal of comfort. Many sensitive people will save themselves a lot of emotional pain and anxiety if they could only grasp this: if your actions or words are from a place of love, or kindness, or even naivety without any intention to harm the other, you are not responsible for how your words or actions make the other feel. No one has that much power over the other. We only have such power over ourselves.

When you're willing to listen and to learn, you realise that the Universe is constantly teaching you. I was called on a duty visit at work to a family who were struggling with the father's recent diagnosis of an autoimmune disease which affected his emotional responses. As I was leaving the visit, I said to God in my mind: *"Why do people have to get sick?"*

I prayed that this father would be helped by Spirit to re-connect to his Truth within him because I knew if he could do that then he would find a special strength that would get him through anything, and then before I even finished my thoughts, Spirit said: *"You can help to heal him."*

"Don't be so ridiculous," I said, without words, and then I was shown that we can help to heal people by looking at them as though they are the single most important person in the world. If we can focus all of our energy on to the one person we are spending time with in any one moment, we are allowing our Truth within; our spark of God within to come forward and this helps their spark to come forward and, with that, there is healing. Not necessarily miraculous healing overnight: in some

cases, it could be miraculous healing but in most cases it will be subtle. I have learnt that in most cases, God's approach is very gentle and nurturing, but this alone is more than enough. Likewise, it may not be physical healing but the most profound and beautiful healing is from the inside. It might include releasing a burden of guilt, anger, fear or resentment that someone has carried for many years. This can be emotionally and physically debilitating and releasing that single emotion may make a person's life much more joyous, in which case they are increasing their frequency and getting closer to their Truth within. However, we must not put pressure on ourselves to heal anyone.

We can treat all people as if they are the most important person in the world and we can love every person unconditionally. This way we are planting a seed of strength – perhaps it gives their healing the boost it needs to get started – but, if that individual is not willing to take responsibility for their own wellbeing and healing, then they will not heal, at least not in the long term. They may experience a temporary healing but, if they are not willing to acknowledge it and to work with it, they will lose it and they will go back to their old habitual ways of thinking and being which made them sick in the first place. I have learnt from my work that many people look to anyone to fix their lives but they do not look to themselves; they do not know the power they hold over their own life. No one can save you; you cannot save anyone. We can only save ourselves.

It is very important that we all have the time and space to grieve, grieving alone enables the healing process. However many people get stuck in the grief stage, we are not supposed to stay there; we are supposed to move forward and, when we do, we begin to learn the lessons grief was destined to teach us. One of two things can happen. One: people do not give themselves time to grieve and so the emotions are not processed and released, they are simply ignored and manifested in other harmful ways. Two: a person grieves but holds on to the emotion as they believe it is all they have left of their loved one, or they believe they are entitled to feel sad, angry, bitter, etc. for the rest of their life; or they feel guilty for releasing their grief. Your loved ones in Spirit do feel sad when you grieve – I have been shown it and I have felt it. They want nothing more than for you to be happy and to move forward with your life. If you can find some positivity from their passing, or make a positive change in your life because of their passing, then they will feel so happy and so proud. The best way you can honour your loved ones in Spirit is to live life with love in your heart and to learn as much as you can whilst you're here on earth.

I have known people who have become obsessed with wanting to communicate with their loved ones in Spirit, to the extent that they have become poorly and have unintentionally neglected the people on earth who need them. We can allow ourselves to have that relationship with our loved ones in Spirit but we must not become consumed by it and we must not rely on it. I used to be obsessed with texting those psychic medium chats until my dad visited me in a dream and told me I must stop texting them. So I rang my network and asked that they block these numbers. I thought that it was only the odd £2.99 here and there but I imagine if I reviewed my statement and took note of how much money I was spending per month on these text messages, it may have amounted to a significant cost. We each have our own journey: there are times when our loved ones in Spirit have to go and do their own thing for a while but remember their love is forever with you. We must fulfil the duties we came here to fulfil; this is the most important thing to the Soul. The reason I have such a strong connection to Dad is because I have found peace in the death of his physical form. I have let him go. By letting him go I have no expectations, and therefore I am not causing energy blocks so it is far easier for him to connect to me. It is so important that we go on with our lives after our stint of grief. **We must love forever but we must not mourn forever**.

Forgiveness

"Forgiveness is to set a prisoner free, and to discover that prisoner was you." – Lewis B. Smedes.

One of the burdens people carry is the inability to forgive those who have hurt them. There are three ways people react to this.

The first is the Reactor. This is the obvious relationship breakdown; there is no communication and the betrayed is clearly angry and makes the betrayer aware of their wrongdoing any chance they get. They feel their anger is justified and they want this person to suffer.

The second is the Faker. This person pretends that they're over it, even acting as though it never happened, seemingly continuing their relationship with the betrayer but, deep down, harbouring resentment towards them: talking negatively of them behind their back; secretly revelling in their hardships; perhaps organising friendship gatherings and 'forgetting' to mention it to them. Like the Reactor, the Faker feels their resentment is justified. The resentment gradually builds up, causing an inevitable explosive rift, resulting in more pain and conflict than would be the case had the original act of betrayal just been acknowledged.

Third is the Wise Man. This person recognises that the Reactor and the Faker are only causing themselves more pain, and has a genuine desire to forgive the betrayer and to move on, not for the benefit of the betrayer but for their own sanity. Sometimes the Reactor and the Faker get to this point – as they mature they become more aware and recognise that their unforgiveness is as punishing to themselves as it is to the betrayer, if not more so. It becomes a burden they do not want to carry anymore. This is a really important first step: to love yourself enough to want to forgive those who have hurt you. But, more often than not, we find that forgiveness does not come when we simply decide we want to forgive, and that brings with it another challenge: *'Why can't I forgive them?'* In this case, we must be so careful not to develop guilt and self-blame: *'I must be a bad person because I can't forgive.'* With this new found awareness and empathy, we may feel especially bad if the betrayer is genuinely trying to make amends. Acceptance is the key to healing in any circumstance, and therefore you can say: '*I don't forgive them, and that's OK.*' This doesn't mean you continue to feel angry or resentful; it means when those feelings arise, you allow them to be. But, you do not react outwardly or inwardly as a reaction would feed the emotion and therefore encourage it to manifest and to grow. When you begin to allow an emotion to be – but to not define you – you allow the natural flow of energy, (that is to feel and to release; energy is not supposed to hang around for more than a moment). Feel, allow/accept, release: there is no should or shouldn't about it. So when you begin to accept your unforgiveness as it is and not as you expect it to be, you find that forgiveness naturally follows suit. Some find that forgiveness enables them to rebuild the relationship stronger than before, but forgiveness does not mean you must allow someone back in to your life; it means you have finally let them go.

It is only natural to feel dislike or anger towards a person, especially if they have hurt you or someone you love. Something that Spirit has allowed me is to feel the pain of the person I have disliked, which has turned my resentment into compassion and love. I had some feelings of dislike towards a woman who had hurt someone I was very fond of, and who was continually spreading rumours about this person. I knew this feeling was so far removed from my Truth within, so I asked Spirit to help me to be able to love this person, even though she was not being very nice to the person I cared for. Around four months into this, I had a dream where I was observing this person in her family home. She was having a firm talking to by a member of her family. As I watched upon them, I maliciously thought to myself: *'HA, I am glad she's being put in her place.'* As I thought this, I was overcome with feelings of such grief and sadness; I felt as though someone had ripped my heart from my chest and was squeezing the air out of it. It was a heartache like I have never felt before; it took my breath away. I knew in that moment, I was experiencing what it feels like to lose a child. As I came to and realised I was safe in my bed, this feeling began to fade and I was incredibly relieved to know that this pain was not my own. I spent a moment reflecting on what I had just experienced. I recalled being told a while ago that this woman had miscarried a child but I had not realised the impact this would have on her. I silently prayed to God: *'Please don't ever let me lose a child.'* I knew I could not bear to feel that pain a moment longer. Whilst this woman's pain was not an excuse to be cruel to the person I cared for, I had a newfound understanding of why she behaved the way she did. I had a newfound connection to her. I had shared her pain: how could I not love her?

This happened again with another two people I was struggling to empathise with but thankfully these were not as painful. I had developed some resentment towards a manager at work who I felt had taken a dislike towards me and favoured some of the other staff. Whilst I was relaxing into a mediation, I was taken into a vision where I was shown my manager walking into a tiny cave, curling herself into a ball, and hiding. My heart ached as I could feel how desperately unhappy and trapped she felt in this job. In fact, my actions were a part of the reason that she did not enjoy it. I had no idea that I was partly responsible for her dislike of me, and I felt such guilt and sorrow for my behaviour. This completely changed my relationship with my manager and even though I have since changed job roles, I still regularly pray for her strength and wellness.

On another occasion, I was struggling with someone close to me who had experienced a dip in her mental health. She deflected this on to all those close to her by being spiteful and rude. I was shown her naked and trying to cover herself in plasters, whilst all those close to her watched upon but did nothing to help. She was trying to fix herself but in reality, rather than asking for help, she was pushing her loved ones away. I asked that I would be able to love all of these people unconditionally, but I also asked that they would be able to love me, as we should never allow anyone to mistreat us because we have compassion for them. We are not doing anyone any favours by making excuses for their behaviour. The saying, 'Hurting people hurt people' is true in some cases and we have to put boundaries in place to protect ourselves. However, that does not give us an excuse to be cruel or to meet these people with as much anger as they are putting on to us. This only makes us equally as accountable and escalates an already difficult situation. In most cases you will find, as I have done, when you meet people with unconditional love, compassion and forgiveness, they tend to meet you halfway and they tend not to mistreat you; it is very difficult to be cruel to those who radiate love.

Whilst writing this book, Spirit showed me some people who have done what we perceive to be very bad things on earth and some of whom are serving a sentence on death row. Spirit helped me to see these people through God's eyes and to understand that this book is destined to find these people and bring them comfort, as much as it is to help the people who are victim to the crime. God loves everyone, even those people who commit crime and cruelty. God loves everyone forever and He has a place in Heaven for all. He only asks that these people develop sorrow and compassion for their act. If a person develops true sorrow and compassion for their act here on earth, they are forgiven and have no need to fear repercussion in the afterlife. However, if they do not care for their act and their victims here on earth, then they will experience repercussions in the afterlife. Spirit will do all they can to help this person feel remorse so that they can grow and be free from the act. If they cannot develop sorrow and compassion for their act even with lots of help in the afterlife, then they will not go to Heaven and this makes God very sad because we are all His creation, and He wants us all to reconnect to our Truth so that we can return home to Him.

Guilt can be a very debilitating emotion, and so when we have felt the sorrow for our actions we must learn to forgive ourselves, even if the victim cannot forgive us because this unforgiveness can also impact how we transition to the afterlife. This also applies to the victim, who may want to forgive the perpetrator and may even feel that they are a bad person for not being able to forgive. Many people who carry guilt feel that they are not worthy enough to go to Heaven or fear what God may do or say to them. And so they turn away from the light. However, please know that God will never make you feel inferior; we only do that to ourselves.

You must never worry about your loved ones in Spirit, for they are always loved and protected. Everything we experience is necessary for our Soul's development and to ultimately find our way back home, back to God. I had been worrying about a gentleman who had become addicted to alcohol and although he had a very beautiful Soul, when he drank alcohol he would become very violent and hurt his family. Spirit took me into a vision whereby this man was a black ball of energy surrounded by lots of beautiful, bright glowing energy. I understood that the bright glowing energy was multiple Spiritual Beings and they were circling him with so much love and protection. I felt they would do this for him for an eternity. Even though he will have to feel the pain he caused his family, in this lifetime or in the afterlife, he will always be loved and protected and when he is able to have compassion for himself and for his family, he will be released from the pain and he will feel those energies of pure love.

The Purpose of Life

What is the purpose of life? I imagine most people have asked themselves this question. This is how Spirit explained the purpose of life to me; they taught me in a way that they knew I would understand because it relates to my life experiences.

Spirit showed me that life is like going to college or university. Our parents support our dreams to go to university to study a subject we are passionate about so that we can pursue our dream to become the person we aspire to be. Whilst at university we make lots of bad decisions that are harmful to our body such as partying too hard, promiscuity and unhealthy eating. Still, some of us will flourish and pass university with flying colours; some of us will pass by the skin of our teeth. Some of us will decide it's not for us and depart prematurely and some of us will fail. Either way we will all return to our parents more grown up and a little wiser. Our parents will look proudly on as we share our newfound knowledge; they will not love us any less should we pass or fail but will be relieved we are home with them where we belong.

God loves us so much that He allows us to come to earth to learn and to develop our Soul. Whatever happens, we return home a little or a lot wiser. God will look proudly upon as we share our newfound knowledge and He will welcome us home with open arms.

We all have lessons that we are destined to learn and whilst we are always loved and accepted back home, it is very sad for the Soul when they leave this earth having not fulfilled their purpose. Often they feel very disappointed in themselves. As always these Souls are very well supported by Spirit who will help them to see that in actual fact they did learn many things, even if it wasn't specifically what they had hoped to.

For many years before Spirit helped me to understand life, I believed my purpose was to be an independent career woman, empowering less fortunate people. I worked very hard to achieve this. I acquired a lot of student debt and spent any money I earned on higher education. Two weeks after I qualified, I had a harsh epiphany whereby I realised that I was motivated by status and money and neither would fulfil me. I realised that it was not the career that was my destiny but the lessons that would be learnt within my career. Initially this was a hard pill to swallow and I completely ignored it for a few weeks. I couldn't stand to think that I'd invested so much money into this specific career with the false belief that I needed wealth and power, when I could have left school and walked straight into a job, and learnt the lessons years earlier. However, when I began to accept this epiphany, I appreciated that it was a great relief to learn that I didn't need to put so much pressure on myself to fulfil this career. Following this realisation, I was able to do my job much better because I was working from my heart. I was not motivated by fear of not meeting the deadlines, fear of losing my job, hierarchy, or a pay rise because I did not care for status or money anymore. I started to enjoy simply *Being* in my job, taking it day by day and appreciating all the opportunities for learning. I also realised that I was not ready to begin employment when I first left school and that those years at university were necessary for my Soul's development.

Indian speaker and writer, Jiddu Krishnamurti once said: "*Do you want to know what my secret is? You see, I don't mind what happens.*" When you begin to understand that you are eternal, nothing scares you anymore because you know you will always be OK. And when you are not worried about things going wrong, things don't tend to go wrong, though if they do, you have such a sense of inner peace that they become right – they become a part of your destiny. When I released my former expectation of my career and the false fulfilment I believed it would bring me, I found a peace within whereby I enjoyed my job but I did not care if I lost it either.

At another time in my life I believed the purpose of life was to make the world a better place, and to sacrifice myself to help as many people as I could. Spirit took me into a vision where I was looking at two earths: one earth was dim, unclean and overcrowded and the other was bright, beautiful and with just as many people, but there was plenty of room for everything. Spirit told me that humans choose which world they live in. I understood that both earths were the same earth but they were people's different perceptions of it. I was told that the majority of humankind perceives the earth as the former: dim and overcrowded. I realised that it is not the earth that needs saving, it is my perception that needs saving. We all share the same purpose and that is to bring love to humanity. If we were all to go within and work on our inner selves, to allow our true self, our spark of God within to step forward and work through humanity, then humanity would not need saving. Love as we know it here on earth is very different to love in Heaven. Here it is conditional; it feels rushed and excitable. But love in Heaven is a feeling of calm, peace and adoration no matter what. It is simply a way of *Being*; there are no conditions attached. This is the goal of the Soul in the human body, to bring that kind of love to humankind so that love is not conditional but rather a state of Being, so that humankind itself is love. We are also here to learn and we need challenges in order to grow, but challenges can be met with love; it is how humanity perceives the challenge that is the problem. We resist challenge and we argue: *'This is not how it should be.'* Therefore we cause ourselves suffering and we attract more hardships. If we were all to embrace the challenges and accept them as a part of our journey and evolution, then they would be overcome far more quickly. A challenge does not include exploitation, murder and other unspeakable acts of cruelty; these are never in anyone's destiny, to inflict or to be inflicted. However, God and Spirit will start shifting events and energy for you so that some hope and positivity can come from that event. Many people make choices that are good for their Soul's development following a tragedy, or they develop a level of compassion and empathy that they never had before the tragedy. **God is always on your side; God is always trying to unfold events to help the development of your Soul**. However, the mind is easily deceived and it will perceive the world exactly how you tell it to. It is entirely your choice as to how you experience life.

Although some of our life path is predetermined, much of our life path unfolds as we go along. There are many lessons that we learn along the way, and these are determined by the choices that we make every day and in every moment. The choices we make here on earth are very important; every choice manifests lessons and consequences. I was shown this when I was thinking about my pet canary, Cosmo. I had purchased Cosmo from a breeder to befriend a finch that I had rescued and hand reared. Sadly they did not get along and so I had to buy Cosmo a separate cage. A few months later, a pet shop surrendered two finches to me as one of them was sick and they were not profitable. So, my mum's small home was quickly becoming overrun with animals. I was considering re-homing Cosmo to a couple I have known since childhood who love animals and who had shown an interest in my finches. I knew I could check on him regularly as they live close by and so I was confident that if there were any problems, I could take him back. I considered that it was OK to rehome Cosmo because I actively looked for him, unlike my finches that were rescues. I had believed that because they had found me, they were destined to be with me but Cosmo was not. As I was considering this, I was taken into a vision where I was back at the breeders choosing Cosmo. In the moment I had chosen Cosmo, lots of words came from him and surrounded him. I knew that these words were all the lessons that Cosmo would teach me, and that these lessons were manifested as soon as I chose Cosmo. I did not rehome Cosmo and as I type this, I feel guilty for even considering it. Cosmo is such a cheeky character; he has brought so much joy in to my life.

Every moment of every day we are given choice: we choose our words, our actions and our thoughts. However, we tend to forget this; we believe we are trapped in a job we do not like because we need to pay bills we do not want to pay, forgetting that we chose the job and we chose the bills. Most of us are stuck in a habitual routine of thinking and doing so much so that we are completely unaware that we have choice. This is a great flaw in humankind; we limit ourselves so much, and we seem to be set on making our lives a misery. *'I want this, but now I don't, but I'm going to keep it anyway because I have to be miserable, even though I can choose to be happy.'* It is really quite bizarre. Whilst we may not always be in control of our circumstances, we always have a choice as to how we respond to them. We can choose to be miserable, angry or resentful, or we can choose peace. So a large part of our purpose on this earth is determined by our everyday choices; making a choice in itself is a life lesson. We may have many paths before us; how our life unfolds depends on which path we choose to take and that will have an impact on all the beings that cross that path. Whilst God may wish for us to make particular choices, and whilst our Soul may have agreed a pre-determined plan before coming to this earth, we may choose not to follow that in human form. We hold the power of our own destiny. This is the gift of free will.

We are condition when we are very young to block out the spark of God within, and ignore our true self, so our primary purpose is to: a) access that spark of God within and allow His unconditional love to step forward; and, b) learn the lessons we came here to learn; not necessarily in that order. *How do we do this?* In order to unlock a) and b) we must simply be alive in every moment; we must be present in all that we are doing. We must be aware of ourselves as Spiritual Beings in human form, but that does not mean we should not help others whilst we are here. Everyone has a destiny. Everyone comes here with a plan but many people lose their way and so God will guide them to the light; in some cases you will be the light.

Chapter 7

Energy Sparkles

When I was around twenty-six years old I started to see energy. Firstly, I would see beautiful gold sparkles, like star dust surrounding people or just in the open air. Sometimes it will be tiny sparkles and other times it will be big and obvious, more like balls of gold light. I was supporting a family who were going through a very challenging time; the parents and the children had to live separately for a while and would spend time together at a family centre supervised by Children's Services. On this occasion, I was supervising the family time, when it was time to say goodbye, the children became very emotional and the parents were trying to comfort them. As I watched the parents embrace their children, I began to see gold sparkles surrounding the whole of the family; almost as if someone had sprinkled fairy dust on them, but not small delicate fairy dust, it was large obvious fairy dust. The sparkles were circling the family but in no particular rhythm. I blinked a few times before the sparkles began to gradually fade away. I am not entirely sure what these gold sparkles are but I know that they have a connection to Angels and I believe they were comforting this family at that moment. After a while, I started to see colours around peoples head or specific body parts, these are normally pink, blue, purple or green and this always happen spontaneously. I know that these colours are linked to a person's aura but I don't see the colour surrounding the whole body; perhaps I could if I spent more time practicing. Spirit also uses specific colours to communicate with us. The Archangels each have a colour that they identify with; I know when Archangel Michael is with me because I will see his blue energy. My dad also often uses the colour blue but he uses a lighter tone than Archangel Michael.

My favourite experience so far, of Archangel Michael's blue energy is when I was out on a walk; I am constantly in communication with Spirit especially when I am in nature, and I often feel Spirit walking with me. On this particular day, I could feel energy to the left of me, so I looked towards it and I smiled as I saw two large blue feet walk one in front of the other. I had initially thought this was Dad but Spirit later told me this was Archangel Michael, and that I am not acknowledging Archangel Michael as much as I should be.

Do you ever notice that you will look right or left or ahead of you at just the right time? This is Spirit guiding you. Spirit finds lots of creative ways to communicate with us and show us they are around us, but our logical mind often gets in the way and people ignore such things, and may even completely forget the experience. Miracles and magic surround us every day but we are so caught up by stress and worry that often we don't even see it. I am still learning myself but Spirit are constantly reminding me of the importance of being in the present moment, as I type this blue sparkles have brushed across my screen; I believe this is Dad reinforcing the importance of being in the present moment. Often we are sat in a room but our mind is still at the office and we can miss out on so much, the world will just pass us by and before we know it all of the opportunities are gone; our children are grown, our parents have left their physical form and we weren't really there for any of it. We know very well that our physical body can be in one place and our mind in another, like when you are driving and before you know it you've reached the destination and you can't even remember how you got there. The most important moments of our life are those simple everyday delights, such as walking the dog, reading the newspaper or collecting your child from school. I have a house bunny and I get up at six thirty a.m. to spend an hour with her before getting ready for work, Spirit remind me that this is sometimes the most important part of my day and I must appreciate and enjoy this very moment and not think about the day ahead. Often we are so focused on our next steps that we miss the magic that is unfolding right in front of us. You may hate your job, but there will be at least a couple of hours before or after work where you can do something you enjoy, like going for a walk or talking to your partner. Also, if you choose to tell yourself that you hate your job then you will continue to find plenty to hate about your job, and in the process you will miss the opportunities for growth, and you will not notice the good things about your working day; for example helping a colleague who is having a bad day, a lunch break sitting in the sunshine or your own achievements within your work tasks.

The most profound vision Spirit have shown me was during a reiki treatment, where I was shown my whole life on earth as if it were happening in seconds, as if we are here one moment and gone the next. It wasn't a life review but rather I felt my life pass me by as if it were a shooting star; I was the shooting star but I was also the galaxies and space surrounding the shooting star. I was shown and felt that our time on earth is so brief and almost irrelevant when compared to the Universe and our forever existence. Of course I know life is a gift and we are all here for a reason or we wouldn't be here at all however, this vision taught me that we are not to take life too seriously; to understand that life is so brief it comes and goes, so appreciate every moment, even the challenges as a gift and for what they are; lessons to be learnt. To view life as an adventure rather than a struggle, because ultimately our struggles are our greatest lessons and they are so temporary that they barely matter at all when compared to the grand scale of our unlimited existence. If we can be absolutely present in any moment, instead of worrying about the past or the future, we will start to be more aware of the temporariness of the moment and therefore we will revel in the good moments and we will not worry about the not so good moments. The insignificance of my life made me feel that it is OK to make mistakes because there is no right or wrong; it's all about the experience. If we can learn from the mistakes then they are perfectly as they should be. Mistakes are very different to conscious decision making where it involves causing harm to another being. Some people make tragic mistakes like choosing to look at their phone whilst driving and unintentionally causing a road collision resulting in the death of another person; this is the most tragic mistake but there was no intention to harm a person within that. This may not feel insignificant to the family members of the bereaved, the driver who unintentionally caused the accident, and to the person who lost their life however, on a higher level, your Soul knows that you are only here for a very short time and so whilst this may feel like a tragedy whilst you are in physical form, your Soul will search for what it can learn from this tragic mistake. The lesson is of most importance to your Soul because then it can take this lesson home with it to support its development. Your Soul knows that you will be home back in the arms of God and eternal peace in a moment; this is inevitable to the Soul.

Spirit took me in to the story of a woman who was grieving the loss of a baby that was never born, she had made a decision over twenty years ago that she later mourned as a tragic mistake and had since married and had grown up children. She had regretted so much that she was never able to nurture this child and watch him grow. I always believed that children who passed away grew up in the Spirit world but Spirit showed me that this baby would remain a baby until his mother passed so that she would be able to nurture him and watch him grow in the Spirit world. I have chosen to refer to this baby as 'he' but I was shown the baby without a single sex; I was shown the baby as 'he' and 'she' which suggests the baby went to the Spirit world before he was given a gender. There is no concept of time in the afterlife so waiting to see a loved one isn't like waiting at all; although this mother had to experience a lifetime on earth before she could see her baby again, the baby only waited a moment. Equally, although raising this child in Spirit would take a lifetime on earth it would only be a moment in the Spirit world, but this mother and child would experience the joy as much or indeed more swimmingly than they would have on earth. Everyone has their own ideal of what their Heaven would be, and Heaven will include all of their earthy desires if they still have these desires upon transitioning to Heaven. This mothers Heaven was to raise her unborn child and as she had felt sorrow and compassion for her child within her lifetime on earth, she was forgiven by God and her child instantly, but she did not forgive herself; she continued to torment herself throughout her earthly life creating her own internal hell. God has so much love for this mother and He felt her sorrow so deep, that He allowed her the experience of nurturing her child in Heaven.

The Power of Love

Although I feel Dad almost every day, I rarely dream of him in form because he struggles to manifest physical form as he has released almost all of his attachment to his earthly body. However, with the help of my step-dad, Dad found a way to present in physical form in a dream. In this dream I was in a waiting room and I was told that my step-dad would be allowed to come to visit me in his earthly form; on reflection this was a strange thing to say as my step-dad has always visited me in his physical form, but rather it is my dad who does not tend to visit in form. Still, in this moment, I accepted what I was told and I didn't even think to question it. I waited for a moment and then he appeared on his chair, I could see that his body or earthly form was sick and tired but his Spirit was very much at peace. This in itself was strange because my step-dad has always presented as bright, healthy and full of life when in his earthly form but again, I did not consider this in the dream, I simply accepted the experience and enjoyed the time I had with my step-dad. The love I was experiencing between my step-dad and I in this dream was incredibly strong, more so than it is in our usual visits; it was really a love I have not felt from myself towards anyone before, it was not love as we know it on earth; it was a state of *Being* and my step-dad and I were both a part of this Being as one, but also with our own individuality. This incredible love wasn't a momentary experience, it lasted the whole dream and I was able to be productive whilst experiencing it, though I don't imagine I could function well if experiencing it on this earth plain; I would be walking around with my head in the clouds. I was aware in this dream that the time I was spending with my step-dad was not going to last forever and therefore I was conscious about making the most of every moment. My step-dad and I were both in a state of euphoric love and happiness; I was very aware that every moment was precious and I wanted to make it special for my step-dad. I was pushing my step-dad around in something that may have been like a go-kart, and we both seemed to find this hilariously funny. I knew that my step-dad's earthly form was tired and I could sense it was almost time for him to go back so as always, we lovingly embraced one another. As I hugged my step-dad I realised his belly was not flat like I knew it to be in his earthly body, it was round and squidgy just like my dad's, I looked up at my step-dad and I was confused as to why his face was rounder and he appeared to have two chins, just like my dad. I realised that I was looking at my step-dad's facial features but my dad's body. I didn't really have a reaction to this in the dream, I just accepted it. Before I knew it, I was transported to an in-between space which was preparing my dad's to go back to their level and me to go back to mine. I remember not liking this space very much at all as it was dark and cold, or at least it felt this way in comparison to the love bubble I had just been experiencing with my dad and step-dad. But I was only there for a very brief moment.

As I reflected on this dream the following day, it was quite obvious to me that my dad and step-dad were showing me that they are one and the same, but they still have their own characteristics and that's why the form was a little bit of both. However, because I don't always remember every detail of some of the dreams I have with my step-dad, I do not fully understand this dream yet and I do not know why my step-dad/dad's body presented as tired and weak. Perhaps my step-dad was allowing my dad to use some of his individual energy so that he could facilitate the visit, and perhaps my dad had to significantly lower his energy frequency in order to have this physical experience with me, where we could laugh together and hug one another for the first time in twenty-five years. I know that manifesting physicality is difficult for Spirit, particularly highly evolved Spirits, and therefore this may be why Dad's earthly form appeared weak, more so the longer Spirit holds their energy in a space not suited to their frequency, the more depleted their energy becomes, and so when I recognised Dad was becoming weaker, I knew this meant that our time together was coming to an end.

That incredible love I was feeling from them to me, and me to them and each of us to ourselves, was our spark of God within and that connected all three of us; the love was incredibly profound but it was absolutely equal, there was an abundance of it but no more for one than the other. My step-dad and Dad were teaching me that they and I are one, we are all a part of God but we have our uniqueness too and this uniqueness is very important because it contributes to the whole. When you experience an awakening, and become more self-aware, you develop an incredible love for all beings and you become a compassionate person. Since developing a strong connection to God, I am very aware that I have become a much more loving person, I truly love all beings, and I experience a strong desire to want to help another suffering being. I believe our Souls quite naturally want to help a suffering being because it understands this being is a part of the whole, a part of that we truly are.

It is really quite profound when we think about the power of love; love is abundant, there is enough for everyone and it never gets tired. The only way we can ever truly have an impact on the world is by working on ourselves so that we can realign with God's love within; we might not be able to see it but being in the presence of someone who has aligned with God's love within, is enough to lift a hurting person's spirits and may give them the strength to get through the rest of the day. When you begin to access that spark of God within, people will be drawn to you, particularly people who feel low and lost in this world because they are all searching for God's light; whether they know it or not. God has put a little spark of His love in all of humankind and has sent us to earth to help increase the frequency on earth so that earth can become Heavenly. **We are all God's love at work in the world.** That spark of God's love within, is also known as the Soul. The Soul is what makes us eternal. Your Soul is wise and knowledgeable; it has all the answers you seek; it is infinitely abundant. The Soul does not bear any anger or resentment, it is compassionate and forgiving, it has a thirst for knowledge and new experiences. The Soul is unconditional love, and your Soul loves you very much.

Sadly, many people become detached from their spark of God within. Some people are so detached from their spark of God within, that God cannot reach them; God has shown me that He cannot reach very low frequency beings because He is at such a high frequency. That is why He asks us to work with them for Him; that is not to preach and certainly not to judge, but to simply *BE* when we are in the presence of low frequency beings, to allow God's spark within us to step forward and to love these people unconditionally.

We are all here working for God; some of us do it much better than others but we each have the same potential, and no one is more worthy than the other. I do it through my writing, another may express God through comedy; God loves to laugh and so it makes perfect sense to me that some people access God within through their humour. Many people bring their spark of God within into this earth through music; music evokes feelings of passion, love, peace and certain songs bring back wonderful memories. I have lots of songs on my playlist that help to connect me to Source. So we all have our own unique ways of bringing God's love into this world. I have met few people who have realigned with God's love within but when I do meet them, they unearth something very powerful within me; the impact they have on this earth is incredibly profound. Sadly, they are often highly sensitive and so they feel the pain that is inflicted on this earth by humankind as if it is their own pain. If they are not prioritising their own healing or if they are not aware of their own eternal *Being*, these feelings can be unbearable and some of these pure Souls simply cannot bare it and chose to depart before their time. When I hear of a Soul ending their life on earth, I feel the burden on my shoulders become a little heavier. If only these people who have accessed God's light within knew how important they are; yes, it may make them more sensitive to the suffering of this earth, they may even be labelled weak or 'soft' but they are not weak, they are warriors and humankind will perish without them. Sometimes I can look at a person or walk past a stranger and I will feel their sadness, this can be very difficult but I know that Spirit have influenced this because they wish for me to pray for this person. Spirit know that if I am able to feel the suffering of this person, I will feel compassion towards them, I will open my heart to them and I will wish and pray with all my heart that they will have some relief and joy in their life. A wish and a prayer from the heart is so much more powerful than a prayer without compassion.

Another important lesson my step-dad and Dad were teaching me in this dream is the importance of play and laughter. I remember having such fun pushing them in that go-kart; perhaps my Spirit needed a boost at that time and they were supporting me through this. I am not very playful in my human form, I don't take life quite as seriously as I used to but clearly I am not having as much fun as Spirit think I should be. I am constantly reminded by Spirit not to take life too seriously, we are supposed to enjoy this journey that we are on, and so long as our pleasure is not harming another being, God and Spirit love to see us enjoying life. In most of my visions with God, He laughs; God's laughter sends ripples of love and joy through my Soul and our laughter can do the same for another human being; laughter is infectious because it is joy, and joy is true to our Being. The Soul is naturally quite childlike, it is inquisitive and playful, it is such a shame that we have this conditioned out of us as we grow into adolescence; fun, play and laughter are not limited to children, they are qualities that are very important throughout the whole of our life and Being. Something Spirit has told me is that they wish for me to dance more, in fact they suggested that I dance every day. Dance is a wonderful experience for the human mind, body and Spirit. Spirit and the Angels love to dance, and they love to see us dancing – you will never see a sober person dancing without a smile on their face.

"I Don't Feel Him The Way You Do"

My siblings tell me that they do not have the same spiritual connection with Dad as I do and certainly they have not experienced his presence at the level I have, but I don't believe that I have a stronger connection to Dad than any of my siblings. However, I do believe I have made myself more available to seek and experience Dad's presence because I have prioritised my healing and my personal growth. In my early twenties, it became very important to me to allow myself the time and space to grieve Dad and to talk about Dad. For many years Dad was an elephant in the room; we were all scared to talk about him because of the pain that might arise with those conversation, but I began to initiate the conversations; I wanted to talk about Dad, I wanted to know about his death. Instead of running away from it or avoiding the pain; I wanted to feel it, I wanted to embrace it and to learn from it. I believe my openness and willingness to grow through the 'tragedy' of seemingly losing my dad at a young age is a primary factor as to how I can connect to Dad so strongly today.

Whilst writing this book I have also considered that Dad's first visit since his passing, when he said he had chosen me to be his Angel links to A Father's Love. Many of my epiphanies or spiritual realisations happen when I am driving; this is likely because I am most present when driving. I was driving to the shop when I began reflecting on Dad's final days on this earth; for many years I didn't understand why he just left and didn't leave a letter or something personal from him for my siblings and I. I was actually quite angry about this for some time. I eventually found the courage to ask my mum why Dad never left a letter or a voice recording, she told me that he did not know he was dying when he was. He thought he had more time. She said even when he was bed ridden a few days before he passed away, he told the doctor that he believed he was getting better. I could feel the scenario in my body as I envisioned it; I could feel the emotions of all the people in that room when Dad said those words; the pity from the doctor, the hope my mum was so desperately clinging on to and the genuine naivety from my dad. My heart gave out to my dad; my super strong dad. In that moment I considered that Dad had chosen me to fulfil what he never got to whilst he was here on earth; to relay messages of hope and love to our family that he would have, had he known his time on earth was coming to an end so soon. I considered that God's Angels communicate to humankind on God's behalf so perhaps Dad chose me to be his Angel; to communicate to our family on his behalf. Though I find it quite ironic that Dad should choose me, considering I was the biggest scaredy cat of us all. Dad has shown me that his siblings, who he was so close to, believe that Dad has missed out on his children growing up; he wants them to know, he has not missed a moment.

I was on the phone to my sister when she said to me "*I know Dad is around me, but I don't feel him the way you do*". After a brief chat we said goodbye, I sat in stillness for barely a moment when I felt my dad say to me, "*I will show her I am around her*". I patiently waited for something to happen and sure enough, two days later I received a message from my sister stating; '*I feel Dad very strongly this morning, I'm sure he kissed me on the forehead*'. I thanked Dad for giving my sister this experience and for validating the words I felt him tell me. For some time after this, I was giving out to Dad and God asking that my siblings would be allowed to have the experiences with Dad like I do. I wanted them to know without a shadow of a doubt that Dad still lives on and continues to guide our family. I knew that if they could only feel his energy as strongly as I could, in that moment they would absolutely know he was with them, like I do when he is with me and this would bring peace to whatever was going on in their lives at that time. I had said to Dad in my mind that it was OK for him to not visit me for a while, if that would mean he could focus on strengthening the connection to my siblings. A short while later I had a spontaneous knowing that my dad was around my younger brother. I told my brother a couple of times to be aware of any signs from Dad, but I was disheartened when his response was always that he had not noticed anything. There was no doubt in my mind that Dad was around my brother and I felt sad that he was not able to feel Dad or recognise the signs I knew he would be sending him. I felt an ache in my chest as I envisioned my dad trying to reach out to my brother however, that worry was instantly taken from me as I was allowed to feel that Dad was not sad; my brother was very young when he passed away and he was only just beginning to show an interest in spirituality, and so it may take some time before he recognises Dad's energy.

Dad was especially close to my siblings for around two weeks before he came to visit me directly. I was driving my car to work when I saw him in my mind eye. He was standing on my left side about three steps behind me. Dad told me without words what I already knew; that he is around our family and I must tell them to look out for the signs he was sending my siblings. When I parked up at the office, I immediately sent a message to my two sisters who are also very spiritual. My sisters couldn't believe it as they shared that they both had a very strong connection to Dad the night prior, they knew without a doubt Dad was with them. At this stage, I rarely feel disbelief when my communication with Dad is verified as it has become such a big part of my daily life, there is no longer any doubt in my mind that it is real. Neither of my sisters had shared this with one another until I raised it. I had met my twin sister a couple of days later and asked her to tell me more about her recent visit from Dad; she shared that my younger brother had been doing some maintenance work for her new business venture and he began fooling around, he showed her a magic trick that reminded her of a trick that Dad used to do where he would make the spots on her dress disappear and reappear; she said it was so powerful that it took her right back to the very moment when she was three years old, sitting on Dad's knee and her feelings of disbelief and joy as the magic unfolded; she could feel that Dad was with her whilst she was reliving her childhood memory. Whilst I was not surprised about my dad's visit, I was overwhelmed by what my sister shared; unbeknown to him, it was my brother that facilitated this communication between my sister and Dad. I had believed that my brother was not noticing the signs from Dad however, this shows that he was subconsciously listening to Dad as he was guiding my brother to do that magic trick, knowing it would trigger a memory for my sister. I have no doubt that Dad set up this conversation between my sister and me the very moment he visited me in the car, to show me that there was no need to feel sad because my brother was listening to him all along, even though he didn't realise it on a conscious level. My brother's spiritual journey is only just beginning but I know he will develop well and his awareness of Dad will grow significantly. I have been shown this.

Sadly, we do not have many photographs of Dad and before the experience I am about to share with you, I had never seen a photograph of Dad with me and my siblings. Today we take photographs all the time, everything is documented on our mobile phones and social media however, when my dad was on earth photographs were nowhere near as popular. I had always held onto a little bit of hope that someday my mum would find a photograph of Dad with us all stored away in a box somewhere. One evening I was relaxing in bed getting ready to fall to sleep when I felt Dad's energy step forward, he said to me *"Someone has a memory of me from many moons ago"*. I intuitively knew this was a photograph or a video. Recently my paternal family set up a family group on WhatsApp and I have reconnected with Dad's siblings and many of my cousins. The day after this experience, I thought to myself *'I should message the family chat and ask if anyone has a photo or a video of Dad'* but I talked myself out of it. Later that day, my cousin shared that he had found some photographs from many years ago. He sent some pictures to the group and joked about the appearance of some of my adult cousins who were young children in the photographs. I scrolled through the pictures and lo and behold, there was a photograph of my dad holding my younger brother, who was a baby at the time, and me and my siblings stood in front of him with my mum crouched down in the middle of us trying to keep us all together; *the first and only picture I now have of my dad with me and my siblings.* I was overjoyed. I shared the visit I had had from Dad in the family chat and thanked my cousin for sharing the photograph. It meant the world to me.

No Such Thing as Coincidence

As Spirit are energy they find it easier to manipulate energy and send us signs via our electronic devices, this can get a little freaky but your loved ones in Spirit never wish to scare you and so if this communication was not a joyful experience for you, Spirit would cease to communicate via this method. I was spending a lot of time at a friend's house when I noted that their television would always turn itself on and off when I was there. My friend had someone look at it but they could not figure out the fault. Not long before this started happening, I had learnt that this friend's mother had miscarried a baby boy late in pregnancy, so I had my suspicions about what was going on here, but I didn't dare share it. A few months after this started happening, I was sitting on the sofa at my home enjoying a cup of tea when I spontaneously started thinking about this freaky television and then I was taken into a beautiful vision. This young man in Spirit who had passed away as a baby showed me he helps his brother at work and he goes for walks with his dad who often speaks to him in his mind. He showed me the family have an item that was kept as a memorial for him but it is rarely used now. As I was coming out of the vision, he showed me his parents and siblings stood together, he was standing behind them and he stretched out his arms so that they reached all around his family (he looked like the children's toy, stretch Armstrong) and then he turned into light surrounding his family but he kept his forearms and hands in human form; I believe he did this to help me understand that he is the light surrounding his family. Unfortunately, I don't yet have the courage to share this vision with the family. Sadly, many people fear Spirit and we may even be accused of being unwell if we share experiences of communication with deceased loved ones. This is something I fear when Spirit nudge me to share an experience; although society is generally more open to life after death and spiritual experience, we are not as far along as I would like us to be.

Sometimes I have an experience with Spirit but I misunderstand the message or even who the Spirit person is. This happened recently when I was in my kitchen cooking dinner when the light in the extractor hood began flickering. I knew there was no electric fault and so I smiled and said in my mind who I thought it was but the light continued to flicker. Not thinking too much into it, I continued cooking when I spontaneously began thinking of a friend who recently passed away; I realised I was wrong, this Spirit person was indeed my friend and not the person I had originally thought it was. To verify this I asked my friend to stop the light from flickering, immediately the light stopped flickering, so I decided to have some fun; I said my friend's name and asked that she make the light flicker again, almost immediately the light began to flicker, I asked it to stop and again it stopped. I said to my friend in my mind, if it is really you make the light do one final flicker. Nothing happened for a good five minutes so I continued chopping the tomatoes when the light did one final flicker. My friend had visited me in a dream a few nights prior to this encounter and therefore I understood her message and thanked her for visiting me. I haven't had a problem with the extractor hood since.

My step-dad also seems to have great fun manipulating electronic devices as a way to show our family he is still around us. When he first passed away the bathroom light flickered a lot, my partner is a very good electrician and he could not find the source, he made a joke that it was haunted. Another time I was on my phone and suddenly my step-dad's name popped up on the screen, this has happened numerous times and totally randomly. One night I was home alone and the television turned itself on, I didn't think too much of it and went to change the channel and again, my step-dad's name appeared on the screen. This is never frightening for me as it is always accompanied by loving energy feels; my step-dad was a cheeky chap and so it is no surprise that his Spirit is having a whale of a time playing tricks on me.

My dad also uses electronic devices to get my attention; there have been a few occasions whereby a song has appeared on my Spotify playlist manipulated by Dad. I was relaxing at home, listening to my 'bird music' playlist which I often leave on all day for my finches. I felt a connection to Source come over me so I closed my eyes and I savoured it (it is such a beautiful feeling of wholeness and love), when an unfamiliar song began to play - I had listened to this playlist on a loop many times so I recognised all the songs on there, and this definitely wasn't one of them. I didn't want to disturb my state of bliss so I did not change the song and I just went with it. The song was 'Beautiful' by Secret Garden. I had never heard this song before but as I listened to the lyrics, I felt Dad's energy step forward, and I felt our energies begin to dance to this song together; every word resonates with the relationship I have with Dad in Spirit. I lavished every moment of the experience, tears rolling down my cheeks. As the song finished, I sat for a moment intent on keeping hold of Dad's energy for as long as I could, and then as if a light shot from the sky into the crown of my head, I was shown I would write 'A Father's Love' and that this would be about my experiences with Dad. I immediately began typing notes on my smart phone; I typed reams and reams and within a few hours I was three chapters in to the book.

This happened for a second time a few months later, though not quite as intensely. I was listening to my 'feel good playlist' and I went to change the song, when I noted a song in the 'recommended songs' called 'Fathers and Daughters' by Boyce Avenue. I had never heard of Boyce Avenue so I initially ignored this and chose the song I had originally planned to listen to. A short while later, I went back to my phone to play some music when I noticed this song again and so I decided to have a listen; the lyrics spoke to my heart, I felt every word as though Dad was speaking them to me himself and again, I had tears streaming down my cheeks and a heart so full of love, I felt it could burst.

It is important to note that I don't have any other songs about fathers and daughters on my Spotify playlists, my playlist is generally upbeat as it is my motivation drive to work on a morning. I considered that this was a strange coincidence; I also considered that there is no such thing as coincidences.

Chapter 8

Mac

When I left university and moved back home, I worked at my sister's cafe which was on a small farm. There were a lot of farm dogs but I took a shine to one in particular called Mac. He was grubby looking, cross eyed, scatty and very clumsy. He was the least favoured dog on the farm, and the only one that slept outside in a barn. I always took a shine to the underdogs so I was naturally drawn to Mac. I often sneaked him sausages, I would collect leftover meat from customer's plates and take it to Mac at the end of my shift. I would sit in the barn with him on my breaks; it was a difficult job at times but a cuddle with Mac always lifted my spirits. I was told by colleagues and my sister that my company lifted Mac's spirit too; his eyes became more focused and he became calmer and more settled. When I was on shift Mac would hang around the door to see me, sometimes he would bolt in and sit at my feet when he caught a glimpse of me, especially when it was thundering, he was scared of thunder.

After two years of working at the cafe, I got a new job more suited to my qualifications. I worried about leaving Mac especially during winter as this was a particularly cold and lonely time for him. I often fantasised about bringing Mac home with me but my mum's home wasn't ideal for another dog as well as our beloved family dog. Between leaving the cafe and starting my new job, I took a holiday with my partner. We were in a restaurant when I received an unexpected message that Mac had passed away. I was heartbroken and I couldn't hold back my tears; I felt incredibly guilty that I never got to say goodbye and I was terrified that Mac had passed away cold and lonely. That night I dreamt that I was making a grave for Mac; I was laying stones over a grave that spelt MAC and as I put the final stone down, I felt my dad's presence, I looked up and a puppy with the exact same markings as Mac ran up to my feet, he was full of love and happiness and I felt him say without words, 'thank you'. This was not the last time Dad brought Mac to visit me in a dream; a few months after Mac's passing, I dreamt of Dad stepping out of a bright white light with Mac by his side, Mac ran up to me but this time he did not stop at my feet, he ran straight into me; in that moment we became one and I could feel how much love Mac had for me. I had always believed that I loved Mac much more than he did me and that the food was a large factor as to why he would wait around the cafe for me. However, in this moment I could feel that his love for me was incredibly strong and unconditional. I woke from the dream to use the bathroom and actually forgot about the dream, as I walked out of my bedroom I was surprised to see our dog on the landing as he always slept in my mum's bedroom, I called out his name and he disappeared, a moment passed and I realised those little pointy ears weren't my dogs, they were Macs. I was instantly reminded of my dream and the love Mac had shown me.

I know losing a pet can be heart wrenching, pets are often our most cherished companion and we are rarely given the time or sympathy to grieve their death. I have never heard of compassionate leave for the loss of a pet. I am incredibly blessed to have experienced what I did with Mac. I was once told that my dad can do a lot more for me in Spirit than he could do here on earth, and it is experiences such as this that remind me what that means. It is very difficult for a parent to see their child sad and there may be times when a parent feels helpless; this also applies to parents in Spirit who will see their child cry for them and their efforts to comfort them go unnoticed. In this instance where I was grieving for Mac, my dad was able to bring Mac to me and comfort me in a way that no one on earth could have.

Pets can help us transition too; a gentleman who I will call Sam, took his own life in his late twenties, he came to me in a dream and he was very unsettled, he kept asking me to tell his mum that he was with her and he would not listen when I was trying to comfort him. Around five months after this dream, I was relaxing in the bath when Sam's face appeared in my mind eye, he was standing at a small arched bridge looking at something, as I looked over the bridge I could see a dog, the dog was gleefully playing, running around in circles and jumping up in the air; I could feel the connection Sam and this dog had with one another and instantly knew he had been a pet at some time during Sam's lifetime on earth. I connected to Sam's thoughts; he was reliving his memories as a child playing with this dog. Suddenly Sam ran over the bridge and toward the dog, as he was running he became a child again. I watched as Sam and the dog faded away into God's light.

Sky and Sunny

I was Christmas shopping with my mum when it suddenly dawned on me that I had to get sand paper for my finches, rather than wait for Mum to finish in the shop which is what I would normally do, I decided I would call straight to the pet shop and meet her later on. As an animal lover, I struggle to go into pet shops as I feel the sadness of the animals, but for some reason this wasn't even on my mind when I decided to have a look in on the animals that were for sale. I was immediately drawn to a white Bengalese finch that was clearly unhappy; she was showing all the signs of sickness and could hardly hold herself on the perch, her mate would try to pull her head up with his beak whilst it would droop, almost as if she was going to tumble off the perch. I spoke to the shop keeper who agreed to have her checked over by the Vet. I rang the following day to find out how she was and I was told that the Vet could not find the cause of her sickness, so the keeper offered for me to take her and her mate free of charge. I lived with Mum at the time and she had already accommodated my house rabbit, a canary and a finch that I hand reared from a few days old, so it took some convincing for her to agree to let me bring these finches home; I named them Sky and Sunny. I put them in a hospital cage where they would be kept extra warm, have lots of vitamins and listen to relaxing bird music. It was important that their space was calm, warm and therapeutic. It was a few days before Christmas and I hadn't actually expected Sky to live to see Christmas, so I sent lots of Christmas wishes out to the Universe and I asked my reiki practitioner, Nicki and my family to send Sky healing. Within a day Sky found the strength to hold herself on the perch which meant she was finally able to rest, as previously she had to keep shaking herself awake so that she would not fall off the perch. Sky spent the first few days eating and sleeping and Sunny began singing, rejoicing that his mate was healing.

I learnt that Sky is an incredibly sensitive bird, and she had been depressed at the pet shop which was making her physically sick. She had been asking God for help and I was the answer to her prayer. It took nothing from me to help Sky and Sunny but it gave Sky hope; a new lease for life and it gave Sunny more time with his love. It gave me so much joy watching Sky grow in strength every day; seeing them happy was the best Christmas gift I could have ever wished for. Unfortunately, six months after I brought Sky home, she developed a lump on her stomach which I believed was a tumour, and she became visibly weaker again. Still, she battled on, I was always in awe at how strong

Sky was; no matter what life threw at her, she always had such a will to live. I believe her love for Sunny and her love for food is what got her through; my birds have a very colourful and varied diet because I love knowing that I am feeding them nutritious food. Every morning when I would bring fresh food, Sky would tuck straight in to it. She would often wake through the night for midnight snacks too. I kept Sky and Sunny in my bedroom as it is the warmest room in the house and it meant I could keep a close eye on Sky. Despite her struggle, she would still bathe herself a couple of times a week; people say sick birds don't bathe but she was clearly sick, she just had such a strong will to live and to make the most of her life. When the tumour appeared and she was sleeping much more, I had considered that the kindest thing for me to do would be to have Sky put to sleep, but every bone in my body was screaming 'NO'. How could I just take her life when she was trying so hard to live; and Sunny, how would he cope without Sky? She is his whole world. But equally how could I let her continue to feel unwell when I have the power to end it. During this time I dreamt that I was walking in a wooded area and suddenly I fell down a hole, I was falling through the sky when a large white bird swooped me up and landed me safely to the ground. She was huge, at least twice the size of me, I could not see her upper body but I could see her feet; she had big, strong owl feet. She was holding me in the most loving and comforting embrace. I could feel the burden she was lifting from me; I could feel it physically, as if she was lifting a huge bag of sand from my back. I felt so much lighter; if she had let me go, I might have floated away. Tears rolled down my cheeks as I realised I knew this bird very well, she was Sky. Sky was powerful, strong and very wise in this dream; she had years of knowledge and experience far beyond my own. *Who am I to take the choice of life away from her,* I thought? And in that moment I realised it was never my choice to make, it was always Sky's choice; what a relief! I was told by Spirit not long after I rescued Sky, that Sky and Sunny have a purpose for each other, and that they both serve a purpose for me. Therefore, I understand now that Sky would not leave this earth until she was satisfied that those purposes were fulfilled. Animals have a Spirit form, just like you and I do, and their Higher Self will choose when it is time for them to leave. We can help with this by giving our blessing; animals love their owner so much that they often hold on longer than they need to, to comfort their owners. I would do animal reiki healing on Sky once a week and I always said to her Higher Self that I support her choice to stay here or to pass over, whatever that may be. Sometimes animals choose to stay and suffer a little longer because human love helps to make their transition more peaceful, and may make their next life easier. For example, I had a rescue bird that I had been nursing, I knew it was very sick and would likely pass away. When animals are passing, I keep them very close to me and I pray for them. I was doing animal reiki on this bird and asking that Spirit would take him so he did not need to suffer anymore; he was visibly in pain. Suddenly he became contented but instead of passing, he became full of life. I had never experienced anything like it before; I truly thought it miraculous. I kept him close for a few hours but as he was doing fine, I put him in a warm cage whilst I caught up with some errands. I was devastated when I checked on him an hour later and he had passed away. I blamed myself for putting him down. I was very upset and I was really angry with God; *'why would you give me hope, just to take it away?'*. That night I awoke with a bit of a fright when I felt something small and dense land on my hand (I always sleep on my left side but for some reason I slept on my back with my left hand over my head and my palm open). It sat on my palm for barely a moment and then it flew off; I felt a small gush off wind on my hand when it took off. Spirit was showing me that this bird was alive and well, living another life free from pain or suffering. They taught me that this bird chose to stay a little longer because its Higher Self knew that the longer it stayed, the stronger my love for it would become and this would help it to have an easier life in its next lifetime. As humankind have God's spark within us, we have the power to heal animals, even if we can't see it physically, and the more we love them, the stronger that healing is. If animals have a traumatic passing, this energy can stay with them and impact their next life but if a human is able to help to heal the animal from that trauma and to love it unconditionally, its next life will be more freeing and more loving. We think that animals are not agents of their own life but Spirit have taught me that there is so much more to animals than humankind realise.

Coincidentally, two days after I amended the book to include Sky's story, she passed away. The night before she passed, I had a restless sleep. My alarm went off at six a.m. and I felt that I had only just got my head on the pillow. Before I fully opened my eyes, I saw one of my Guides, Zeus; he didn't say anything, he just stood there looking all serious. I noted that he was wearing a brown robe, which was different to the blue wizardry gown he normally wears but I didn't think much of it. I just marvelled at the impressive long beard he has; I never tire of it. I know that Zeus's role is to help me connect to animals but I did not know Zeus's role that day was to take Sky home to the spirit world. Spirit did not divulge this information to me until after I buried Sky in the garden. I had never considered that there is allocated Spirit people who will guide an animal through their passing, just like there is Spirit people who will guide humans through their transition to Heaven, but indeed there is and isn't that just so beautiful.

The following morning, I awoke thinking of Sky. I had a sickness feeling at the pit of my stomach that would come and go; I was grieving. I wondered how Sunny would feel waking that morning without his mate; the nausea intensified and then I was transported into a vision. Sunny used to always wait until Sky had her breakfast before he began eating but this morning there was no Sky. I was shown a vision of Sunny eating his breakfast and I was allowed to feel his confusion and sadness surrounding Sky's absence. Behind him I could see Sky jumping from perch to perch full of youth and life; as she was elderly when I rescued her, I had never seen her with so much energy. I knew Sunny could not see her like I could; I don't know why that is, I guess his energy frequency is too low or perhaps the vision was more for my benefit. Sky came back to see Sunny for a moment, and she will continue to do that whenever she wishes. Just like our family in Spirit can visit us on earth, our pets can too. God wants us to know this and this is why He has allowed me to experience it.

A few days after Sky passed, I began looking for Bengalese finches to rehome; Bengalese are a sociable breed and I knew Sunny would become depressed without companionship. It would be almost three weeks before I found a pair that needed to be re-homed. I was only looking for a female but I did not want to separate the pair so I agreed to take them both. Although Bengalese are generally very sociable and friendly, I had fears that because they were a pair, they may not take to Sunny and they may leave him out. I gave out to God a lot about this, asking if I was making the right choice and praying that this pair would love Sunny. Sunny had not been himself since Sky passed, he would normally rise at around seven a.m. and he would always sing; that was my cue to take the blanket off the cage. However, he had stopped singing in the morning and I would have to wake him. The day that Sunny's new friends were due to arrive, Sunny awoke at seven a.m. singing his little head off, I lifted the blanket from his cage and he was excitably hopping from perch to perch, just like he used to do. He was in such bright spirits that I said to my mum *"it's as if he knows he has some new friends arriving today"*. My sister was collecting the birds for me as the breeder lived close to her home city which is a two hour drive away from my home. It was just after eight p.m.

before she arrived and Sunny was still wide awake tweeting and flapping around. He would normally settle to bed at around seven-ish and I would cover the cage at around seven thirty p.m. but since Sky had passed, he had been going to bed much earlier at six-ish. So I couldn't believe he was still wide awake and full of energy. The advice is to quarantine new birds for two weeks in case of illness but my sister had no worries about the environment the birds came from, and I gave them a thorough check over, so I was confident they were in good health. Not wanting to upset Sunny's spirits, I put the cage with the new birds, Storm and Snow next to Sunny's cage so they could see and hear one another before I put them to bed. The next morning Sunny awoke at seven a.m. singing his morning song, I was equally excited so I jumped out of bed and immediately moved Storm and Snow in to their new home with Sunny. It took no time at all before they were all eating together and cuddled together on the perch. As I sat and watched them, my heart full of love and relief that my old boy, Sunny had his happiness back, I saw a bundle of gold sparkles sprinkle in to, and throughout the cage; it was as if someone had poured a bucket full of gold fairy dust over the cage and on to the three birds. I knew then that I had made the right choice to rehome both Storm and Snow and that Spirit was congratulating me on this choice. I know that Spirit was showing me that God heard my prayers and He was answering my wishes that Storm and Snow would love Sunny and no one would be singled out, and I also know that those sparkles were a physical manifestation of the love I was feeling for Sunny,

Storm and Snow in that moment and that this love was already having an impact on how the rest of their lives would be.

The Animal Nursery

Just five more minutes, I thought to myself as my partner kissed me goodbye and I tucked my head under the duvet. It was a Saturday morning so I could enjoy the luxury of a lie in, more so my partner had to be away early so I had the whole bed to myself. As I relaxed in bed, I began thinking of Sky, I went into a trans-like state and I could hear Spirit talking to me reassuring me that Sky is OK and that she can come back anytime she likes. I asked God *"will you show me where Sky is?"* and within seconds a beautiful white barn owl appeared in the distance. I decided I would walk towards the barn owl as she may be able to lead me to Sky. As I was walking, I realised I was on a long winding path that seemed to have no end, and I was surrounded by the greenest grass; this grass was not like anything I have ever seen, it shimmered with life and vitality. I looked to the right of me and there were three brown cows, one of which had a bell around its neck. I noted that the cows were also glowing with good health. There was a feeling of absolute serenity, peaceful bliss and eternal safety. I said out loud *"thank you God for allowing me to see this place"*. The cows and the barn owl suddenly stopped what they were doing and looked at me; they gave me a funny look, like it was not my business to be there, if they had spoken, I imagine they would have said *"what are you doing here?"*. I continued walking the winding path when I felt God at the pit of my stomach say "STOP", but curiosity got the better of me and I attempted to continue walking the path. I barely got another two steps in when the path started to dip slightly and I was slipping down it. I knew I had to turn back so I turned around and I pulled myself back up the path, this wasn't easy as it felt like something was pushing against me. I managed to get myself back to where I should be and then I was back in my bedroom. I have a feeling that had I continued to walk that path, I may not have been able to find my way back, or indeed, I may not have wanted to find my way back. I know that in this vision, God allowed me to see a little piece of my Heaven and this is where Sky is; she is in my Heaven waiting for me, and when it is my time to go home, I won't have to turn back.

Just like there are nurseries in Heaven for children who pass away, there are nurseries in Heaven for animals that pass away. Pets bring humans so much love and joy and that love does not just disappear, it is there for us when we go home to Heaven. God loves us so much that He allows our pets to be in Heaven with us; God is overjoyed that we have nurtured and loved another being. Whilst writing the book, I was shown what an animal nursery in Heaven would look like. The animals were surrounded by a small white fence which kept them all together within the nursery, but it would expand as they were playing, so it would be never ending and they would have all the space they needed. There were Angels in there whose job was to care for the animals; I know that pet owners are not with their animals all the time in the Spirit world as they have other duties, and so their animals mostly live in the nursery but their owners would come and go whenever they wanted. Although I do not know a lot about the Angels who care for the animals, I know that they love doing this and that this is their purpose.

My connection to animals has significantly increased since my first awakening. I started to feel their Spirit just as strong as I feel the energy of a human. I cannot stand to see or hear of an animal being cruelly treated because I am so connected to their energy that I feel their suffering. Spirit showed me a vision of animals in a pet shop, they were all in small cages like they are in reality however they were also physically gagged; I understood that this was wrong but the pet shop worker carried on his business as if this was totally acceptable. In reality animals are not physically gagged but they are gagged in every other sense of the word; they are not allowed a personality or freedom to express themselves, they must do as humans expect them to do. Whether an animal has a happy or miserable life is entirely in human hands, we choose the life path of our animals on earth. Sometimes I am taken into a vision where I am with an animal who is suffering, I feel the animals fear as if it were my own, and in every vision it is the human who is the source of the animals suffering. This is very upsetting for me, I used to feel shame and guilt for having these visions and I would try very hard to push them to the back of my mind; I would complain to Spirit 'why would you show me that?' but I understand now that my role is to comfort that animal, to bring it some peace and to take some of its pain away; in which case I am learning to view it as a blessing.

It is very difficult for people who do not have a strong connection to animals to understand the love I have for animals and likewise, it is very difficult for people who are connected to animals to understand how people can treat animals as though their life is insignificant and as though they do not have thought and feel. Like humans, every single animal is unique and they each have their own personality; no matter how big or small, tame or wild, every single animal wants to live a life of love and free from suffering. Animals are nearly always in our life to teach us a lesson; typically the lessons are patience, selflessness and unconditional love. If you choose not to learn these lessons and to treat an animal as insignificant or cause the animal deliberate harm, you will have to learn compassion and empathy for that animal, either in this life or upon your passing before you can go to Heaven. In order to learn compassion for this animal, you will have to feel the suffering you caused it.

On a summer's day in March 2020, my mum brought home a young pigeon that had an open wound from a hawk attack, after a visit to the Vet we agreed to nurse the pigeon and we named her Pip. Pip recovered well and after four weeks we took her to a sanctuary to be rehabilitated back into the wild. Word got out and people began to bring sick birds to me. I received a telephone call about a young pigeon who had fallen from its nest and had been pecked almost to death by hens; the lady who found him originally thought he was a piece of rubbish being flown around by the wind. I named him Zeus, after my Guide. However, I originally spelt it as Zius but a few months later, my Guide showed me that I had been spelling his name wrong and it was indeed 'Zeus'. It is not often that I cuddle the sick birds that I bring home as it can be distressing for them however, I intuitively felt that Zeus needed the reassurance so I sat by the fire and held him as he fell to sleep in my arms. The following morning I bathed Zeus; you know when you're feeling so poorly and you're so grateful for a hot bath, I'm certain Zeus felt this way. He sank into the small tub as I gently massaged the mud from him, I could feel his contentment as he lifted his head and looked at me; he didn't need to speak my language for me to know that he was saying *thank you*. I begrudged having to leave Zeus for work that morning, and you can imagine my heartache when I received the message from my mum that he had passed away. When you develop sensitivity to every other living being, when you have awareness that their feelings and purpose is equal to your own, you feel the loss, it is painful and you grieve. Spirit tell me that there is no such thing as death, even animals never die, they go to the Spirit world or they reincarnate back to this earth. But even after everything Spirit has shown me, I grieve when an animal that is brought to me passes away. I feel that I have failed; I feel that I have let down the individual who brought the animal to me, and I also feel that I have let down the animal. It can be very difficult for me. Still, I was grateful that I was able to make Zeus's passing more comfortable and I'm certain he knew he was loved.

It is so important to listen to your intuition. When Spirit guides you to an animal in need, whether that be an animal that is sick, stuck somewhere it shouldn't be, an animal trying to escape another being whose intention is to harm it; whatever it is, if you are drawn to an animal in any situation where you can help, know that Spirit have guided you to see this and Spirit want you to intervene, not only for the animal but for yourself. When you help any being in need, you are rewarded and your Soul will enjoy looking back on this experience in your life review. Our rewards are magnified when we help a being knowing that they cannot give us anything in return however, the warmth in your heart you will feel when you watch the animal recover or knowing that you have helped it pass peacefully, is incredibly rewarding. You are destined to learn a lesson within that and to fulfil some of your Soul's purpose. Animals are a gift to humankind, we are supposed to protect them; the commercialisation of animals and humankinds lack of empathy towards animals is truly a tragedy and is not in any way condoned by God. I am often degraded for my kindness to animals, I used to feel embarrassed to talk about the animals I rescued; some people laughed at me and made jokes about my newfound love of animals. I was told I was too soft as if it were a weakness. Kindness is not a weakness; it is compassion, a quality that humankind greatly lacks. Everyone possesses compassion deep within and many people do feel it, even just for a moment, but many people do not have the courage to act on it. Compassion is a very basic human emotion and we cannot get into Heaven without it; the more we feel compassion and act upon it, the more we are rewarded; in this life and indefinitely in the afterlife.

Kindness = Abundance

I always ask Dad to help when I am brought a sick animal; our loved ones in Spirit love to be asked for help. They can help us tremendously and we can ask for help with anything at all, but we must be realistic about our expectations. Spirit cannot keep people alive on earth if it is their destined time to cross over, they cannot make you financially wealthy and they cannot bring your ex back however, they can make the emotional hardships that come with these challenges a little easier by setting up a chance encounter, or sending you energetic strength and healing or even visiting you in a dream to tell you everything will be OK. I know Dad answers my wishes for him to help with my animal rescues because I have seen his blue light brush over some of the animals when I am nursing them. They don't all survive but I know that mine and Dad's energy combined has helped to make their transition easier.

I believe Dad set up my first animal rescues; it was at a time I was worrying about money and regularly giving out to Dad for financial abundance. I knew he heard my wishes and was trying his best to answer, because I saw him sat at a big table in a suit talking to my spirit team (my dad was training to be an accountant when he got sick). I patiently waited for the pay cheque to arrive. It never arrived. However, abundance came in the form of my animal rescues. Pip, Zeus and Sky unearthed emotions within me I didn't know I had; unconditional love. The rewards of knowing I am comforting a helpless animal in need far outweigh any need for financial gain. I found that I was so preoccupied with my animal rescues that I stopped worrying about finances; if our hearts could physically grow, I know that my heart would grow ten times bigger since I began volunteering with animal rescues. In those moments I was nursing the animals, I was experiencing internal peace and abundance, and because I was becoming a more loving person, a more loving life came to me. It didn't dawn on me that Dad was the mastermind behind this until nine months after my first rescue and two months post rescuing Sky; I was sitting watching Sky happily chirping away, my heart bursting with love and pride as I reflected on how far she had come from that day I saw her in the pet shop when I was so sure she was going to pass away, and I thought to myself 'this is wealth'. In this moment I saw that vision again of Dad sitting at the table with my spirit team, I felt his energy touch my shoulder and sprinkle down my arms and I knew Dad had been teaching me what wealth and abundance truly is. That is not to say that there is anything wrong with financial abundance, or that we shouldn't ask Spirit for financial help. Spirit may not be able to provide you with financial wealth but they can help to change your mind set so that you are able to attract financial wealth yourself. I will not pretend to be an expert on the Law of Attraction because if I was I would not still be living at my mum's home. However, I do know that what we give out into the Universe we get back tenfold. When we are kind and generous with a pure heart, we will be rewarded. When we are acting from a place of love, we are increasing our energy frequency and therefore we are more likely to attract what we want. Love is the most powerful energy of all, where there is true love there cannot be lack. If you have aspirations to fulfil a career that involves helping people for example, and your genuine desire is from a place of love, then the Universe will begin to shift events in your life so that this aspiration can be fulfilled. If your desire is to make a lot of money because you are angry at the world and you want to gain power and control over people, the Universe is not going to be on your side. If we give from a place of true love, we are always, always going to be rewarded. The problem is many people resent giving, they believe that in order to give they have to lose something; they fear giving love because they fear it will make them vulnerable and they believe vulnerability is a weakness; a loss. God is constantly giving, God's energy is like a constant flow of love that is coming from Him to all that surrounds Him, and nothing goes back into it; God takes nothing, yet God is absolute abundance. However, humankind is at a much lower frequency than God and one of the most important human qualities is self-love, this is also a quality that is almost non-existent on this earth. People either feel guilty for giving to themselves or they give to themselves because they feel bad about themselves. I used to be very good at saving money because I would never buy myself anything or when I did, I would feel guilty for spending on myself. However, I no longer feel guilty for spending on myself. I tend to ask myself three questions; *Do I really need this item? Is it going to last? Do I feel good about it?* If the answer is yes to all three, I spend the money and I feel good about it. If I was to start to feel guilty, I would immediately attract lack. I also give money to charities and people who are homeless. I don't ever worry about giving money because I am confident that it will find its way back to me. In that moment when I am helping an animal or a person in need and my action is from a place of true love, I am already attracting wealth into my life. However, if you are giving from the ego; that is to simply make yourself feel good, worthy or to look good to the people around you, then you will not attract abundance. Abundance is love and therefore a not-love act simply cannot attract true abundance.

I remember a senior colleague of mine told me that my kindness will be thrown back in my face, she gave me an example of a young Social Worker who worked hard to raise money, food and clothes for a less fortunate family at Christmas; the family accepted this gift and appeared very grateful. A few months later, the parents of this family stood in Court and told the judge what a terrible Social Worker this young women was; the Social Worker cried to her colleagues relaying what she had done for the family at Christmas. I hope to always remember this story, not to discourage me from being kind but to remind me what kindness is. Kindness should not carry expectation, we should not be kind with the expectation that we will be thanked or re-imbursed for it. Kindness is the quality of being friendly and compassionate; it is the ability to make a positive impact. If someone chooses to reject your kindness that is OK, this says more about the person than it does about you. People too often fear that a person may reject or take advantage of our kindness. Kindness can be mistaken as naivety or weakness because we think that it makes us vulnerable to humiliation. For example, I gave a gentleman who is homeless forty pound in the belief that this will fund two nights at a hostel, as he told me it would; my friend asked if I was not worried that he may have spent the forty pound on drugs or alcohol. I was not worried because my intention was pure and kind, how this person chose to respond to my kindness is a reflection on them and not on me. Kindness often requires courage and strength because it involves giving some of yourself, it is the ability to put yourself in someone else shoes. This can be particularly challenging in a society that has engraved a 'survival of the fittest' ethos which is associated with selfishness and putting ourselves first. Kind people have mastered the art of self-discipline because their wisdom overrides the need for self-righteousness; it is easy to be rude to a rude man, it is far more challenging to consider the rude man's motives and wish him well. In this situation, who walks away with more power? Undoubtedly the kind person because they have not enabled this man to affect their own emotions, their dignity remains intact and there will be no post guilt. Kindness is a sign of a person who has done a lot of personal work and has come to a great self-understanding.

I do have days where I lose faith in humanity; because of the job I do, I work with families who have inflicted torment and abuse on themselves, their partners, their children and/or animals. Likewise, the News and social media often show stories of people and animals that have been badly treated. This can take an emotional toll and sometimes I feel angry towards humankind. Still, for all the pain in the world, there is always beauty to be found; beauty surrounds us every day and Spirit will do all they can to help us to see it. This particular day, I was having a tough week at work; I felt drained and so fed up, I was giving out to Spirit asking for a break. A few hours after I finished work I received a phone call about three fledglings in a woman's shed. I attended the home with my small cat carrier expecting to have to take the fledglings with me. I was pleased to see that the fledglings were very healthy; their mother had clearly been caring for them for weeks in that shed. I felt it would be so sad to remove them from the shed as they had made themselves at home here, and they were safe from cats and crows and the scorching heat we had at the time. I shared this with the woman prepared for her to argue that they must be removed but I couldn't have been more wrong; I was overjoyed when she said she was more than happy for them to stay and she would check on them regularly. She simply wanted reassurance that they were healthy and that her shed was a safe space for them; she was a great animal lover like me. I left this home feeling so uplifted, my heart so full of love knowing that the little bird family had a safe space to continue to grow until they were fully fledged, and knowing that humankind was a part of providing their safe haven. The woman contacted me a few weeks later sharing that the birds had fledged and she was hopeful that they would nest in her shed again next year. This woman will one day experience the contentment she has allowed for this bird family and the relief her actions made me feel; she will be allowed to experience the wonderful thing she did, and the positive impact this has had on the earth. I can't wait for the day she gets to experience that. When we go home to Heaven, we relive our actions on earth and we are made to feel the impact we had on the earth and how we made others feel; the good times and the bad times. So for all the good that we do on this earth and all the lives we touch with love, we are rewarded in the afterlife. I have been shown that we have pots of gold in the Spirit world, but this is simply a metaphor as materialism is not wealth in the afterlife; wealth is being closer to God.

I know that Spirit setup this encounter just when I needed it; the nest must have been in that shed for at least four weeks and this woman was in and out of the shed daily but had never noticed it or heard the nestlings tweet. I believe Spirit made this invisible to her until they wanted her to see it, knowing that she would call me as I had built a reputation as the local 'bird lady'. Spirit set this up at a time I needed the relief the most, on a day I was feeling so low and losing hope in humanity; they reminded me that most of humanity is beautiful and my day finished on a high, with a heart full of gratitude and love.

Chapter 9

Thank You For Loving Me

As you have read early in the book, my communication with Dad is through my intuition or *energy feels*; I feel his words and this is how we communicate. For example, when Dad told me he was going to show my sister he is around her; it was said exactly like that but felt rather than heard. How do I know it is real? And that it is his words rather than mine? I know because I am given verification through energy feels; when it is Dad I feel him envelope me in a big hug, sometimes he will send a song that resonates, sometimes I share my experience and I am given verification through another person, like when my sisters told me they did indeed have a visit from Dad, and as I learn to trust myself more, I know because *I just know!*

This next visit from Dad was different to normal but no less magical; I was doing a guided meditation, the Guide talks you through the journey but often I get so relaxed I forget sections of the meditation or I go into a vision. I zoned out for a while but then I became aware of the meditation where the Guide was saying "*thank you for loving me as much as I love you*" as he was saying this, I could clearly see my dad in my mind eye, he was standing amongst the Heavenly scenery that the Guide had walked me into, and he was gently smiling at me. It did not matter that the words came in the form of the Guide's voice for I knew they were from my dad. My understanding is that my dad was thanking me for expressing my love for him by acknowledging his presence and more so by writing this book which will ensure that his role as a father lives on, and that his death is not in vain. Sometimes a person may say something to you that is exactly something that your deceased loved one would say or you overhear a conversation and what was said was exactly what you needed to hear; these experiences are not coincidence, it is Spirit working their magic.

There is a lot that Spirit can do for us however, sometimes we expect too much from them. Spirits are not supposed to hold on to their human form in the afterlife, indeed it is a tragedy when they cannot let go of their human-ness. This is not something we are expected to do as soon as we transition, we are walked through it very gently but it is something that must be done in order to progress; if Spirit do not choose to progress they become stuck. When I was first taught that my dad had to let go of his human qualities, I rejected it; I was very upset that my dad might not be as I knew him to be. However, I am aware of the importance of spiritual development, indeed it is an important part of my life and so in time I reflected that it would be selfish to expect my dad to put his development on hold for me. I decided that I love Dad so much that I must let him go. I didn't realise that by 'letting him go', I was actually bringing him much closer to me because I was accepting him beyond the physicality that I remembered him to be. As I accepted this, I clearly understood that my dad's love for me is not a human quality, his love for me comes from his Soul and so that will never leave him, it will be a part of him throughout his development and it will be a part of me throughout my life. Humans think we need physicality to know someone but we do not, people who are in tune with their intuition can feel a person's qualities before they even speak. This is what it is like when my dad connects to me; I can feel everything that I knew him to be when I was a child even though I can't physically see and hear him. I want you to understand this; everything is energy and energy never dies, it is eternal. Love is the most powerful energy of all so when we love someone and they love us, this love never dies, it is forever a part of us; the loved one is forever a part of us as we are them. So even when Dad has to be elsewhere on his spiritual journey, a part of him will always be with me. The love Dad and I have for one another is so powerful and so unconditional, it binds us together forever.

I know that it is very hard to let go of what we know but it is very sad when Spirit remains earth bound for too long. Whilst I am not a medium, I have had experiences where I have helped earth bound Spirits begin the transition to the afterlife, this is something that comes quite naturally to me however, I still do not have a clear understanding of how or why I am able to do this. Please know that this is a part of the Spirit person's journey and they are always safe, loved and protected.

Helping Spirits Transition

I was relaxing in bed when I was taken to a rundown living area belonging to an elderly couple, both earth bound Spirits, both bodies warn and tired. The gentleman, a stubborn man was sitting in an armchair looking straight ahead, his wife was standing behind him; she was frail and timid. The gentleman was not yet ready to let go of his human attachments. I was there to collect his wife however, it was important to her to have her husband's approval before making the transition. I felt that passing over was something she yearned for, for some time but her loyalties to her husband prevented her from making the transition. Her husband reluctantly gave her verbal permission to go, and at that I led her away. It was a beautiful relief for this lady and I watched her return to youthfulness surrounded by light and greeted by lots of family and friends; it was a kind of rebirth. The gentleman was scared to transition because he did not like the unknown, he was a man stuck in his ways on earth and he carried this with him in his death. I have since been shown that shortly after she went to Heaven, his wife came back and walked him through his transition. This couple could have transitioned together but they would have been led by more developed

Guides and Spirit, this gentleman did not trust that process and therefore they were earth bound for too long, it was decided that when his wife was ready, she would transition and come back for him; she was the only person he trusted in life and she was the only person he trusted in death.

We all have a spirit team whom help us plan our life before we are born, and who guide us through our life. They meet regularly and discuss our progress and at times they may need to amend our contract, like in the case of this gentleman's passing. Although he refused to transition with them, when he made the transition, he will have been reminded of their role and he will have quickly become familiar with them. Our Guides are like our family in Heaven, we are just as familiar and fond of them as we are our family on earth.

I first became aware of my ability to help people transition around six months before I started writing this book; the summer of 2020. I would often get snippets of a stranger's life, like I was watching a very short clip of a movie but it never made any sense. The first one I can remember was a soldier, he was lay on the ground playing dead and he was surrounded by deceased soldiers, a solider from the opposition walked up to him and I knew he would shoot him in the head and this soldier would instantly pass away. This was upsetting for me and very confusing; I had no idea why I would experience this in my mind. I had a couple more of these visions before I began to realise that there was a pattern; I seemed to be with people at the moment of the death of their physical body. I knew that somehow I was able to offer these people some relief, so I began to embrace the visions and I found myself observing myself as the expert, even though I had no idea what I was doing. I have so many of these visions that it is hard to remember them all but some of them stay with me, like this one; I was relaxing into a meditation when I was taken to a young man who was wearing a motorbike helmet, I asked why he had the helmet on and he replied that it was to keep himself safe; I knew we were in the afterlife and so I told him, he is safe here and he did not need to wear the helmet, and then I was brought out of the vision. As I was coming back I realised this young man did not know that he had passed away, *'poor Soul'* I thought; I hope someone can help him. This young man stayed with me for a while but was really no bother at all; I only know he was around because my partner and I were decorating my bedroom when I saw a Spirit walk into the room in motorbike gear. I smiled to myself and carried on painting the bedroom wall. Months later, I was out on a run when I recalled a dream I had the previous night of someone handing me a motorbike helmet; I wondered what this had meant when it dawned on me that this young man had made the full transition to Heaven, and he was handing me the helmet to show me he had done it. I do not know what my role was in this young man's transition, perhaps just to tell him that he had passed away. Either way, it was comforting to know that he had transitioned and he had chosen to visit me to show me the progress he had made. Sometimes we don't need to know how we do what we do, we just need to embrace it and be grateful for the opportunity to help another or to witness another's joy.

As I became more aware of my ability to help people transition to Heaven, I was able to play more of an active role in what I was doing instead of just feeling like the observer. I discovered that when it was a particularly hard passing, I could use my special blanket to wrap around the Spirit to help them feel safe. I first discovered this when I saw a man soaking wet, as if he had just been swimming in the lake fully clothed. There was an investigation into a high profile murder case in my area at the time, and the body had been found in a river so I knew who this man was. Without even thinking about it, I wrapped him in a blanket and then I was back in my bedroom. I was reassured that my work was done and this man would be further supported by his Spirit team to help his full transition. I have had a few visions from Spirits who have been murdered, they are the most likely to have trouble transitioning due to their death being so traumatic, they may be confused or hesitant to trust the transition process but know that they are always safe and loved and they get lots of help to find their way back home. I don't know what my role is with people who have been murdered as I don't always witness the transition; often they are showing me their story and I am simply observing. I very rarely remember faces or features during a vision especially a traumatic vision however I can recall the outline of the Spirit person, and I feel the individual's personality including their age and gender. When I first began having visions from Spirits and I still found it a scary experience, I had a young woman tell me her story over three nights; she was murdered by a gentleman whom I knew had murdered two other woman before her. I would wake up in a cold sweat and give out to my Guardian Angel and Archangel Michael, I would ask that they would help me forget the dream and they mostly did however, I would remember parts of it. During my final dream, I could hear the woman calling for help and I knew the call was for me, but I was too scared and so I hid; as far as I can remember, she did not find me. I have not had any more dreams or visions as intense as this one however, I have had a vision of a gentleman who murdered a woman. He was sitting in an arm chair, and he asked me if the heart-attack had killed her; I knew he and another gentleman had beat this woman very badly, and he just needed to know that it was not the beating that had killed her but rather the heart-attack. I simply responded "*yes*" as somehow I knew that it was indeed the heart-attack that had killed this woman however, I also knew that the beating had caused the heart-attack but I was not to say that. This brought this gentleman some relief and he was able to begin healing. I felt a feeling of distaste and resentment towards this gentleman as I could feel his horrific crime however, when I came out of this vision, I reflected that it was not my place to judge. This gentleman was elderly upon his passing and this crime, committed when he was younger had tormented him most of his life. He had developed compassion for this woman, and sorrow for his actions but he rejected his transition because he continued to feel so bad about himself and his actions. My role was to relieve this gentleman of his self-inflicted torment. God loves this gentleman unconditionally; he is God's child as we all are, and God wants him to return home to Him. I know it may be difficult to understand but God has shown me that His love for these people who have committed crime is no less than His love for me and He wishes for them to be helped; these people need the most help because without it, they will continue to commit crime. Likewise, what hope do they have if we all have distasteful feelings towards them, if we all judge them as beyond hope?

Helping Spirit transition isn't always doom and gloom; I helped one lady who was a real character. She was a middle aged woman and was wearing running gear, so I knew she had been a fitness fanatic when on earth. She knew she was dead and she wanted to transition but for whatever reason she had not yet transitioned. She was an impatient lady and really just wanted to get on with it. I suspect she wasn't happy about dying when she did and initially resisted death; our spirit team will do all they can to help the transition between life and death of the human body however, we have free will to refuse this and many people fear it, or do not want to leave earth which causes a disruption to their transition to Heaven. I noticed that this lady had a shadow on and around her knee cap so I knew this was partly responsible for her death. As she was impatiently babbling on, I saw lily pads appear across a river, knowing this was her path to Heaven I told her she must hop along the lily pads. She was not impressed by this but did so nevertheless and was met by her Guide who walked her to the gates of Heaven. I had another young girl who was holding a violin, she was barely with me for a moment when her family appeared and she dropped her violin and ran straight to them; the funny thing was, her violin picked itself up and followed her into the light. This highlights that we can take material objects to Heaven with us; if they bring joy and love to our life, of course God will allow them to come to Heaven with us.

A Visit From My Grandma

Spirit very often visit their loved ones in their dreams, this is my favourite form of communication because I see and hear the Spirit as if they are living, I can hug them and I almost always know that this is a temporary visit so I make the most of every moment. I have spiritual dreams more frequently than not but it is not always a visit, sometimes it is a premonition or a message from Source that is delivered via a metaphor and of course, *feel*. I also have Spirits visit me in my dreams asking that I pass on messages to their loved ones, these Spirits will have tried desperately to communicate with their loved ones to show them that they are with them, but for some reason or another the loved one has not seen the signs or has seen them and has doubted them or dismissed them. The main cause for not being receptive to spiritual visits and signs is energy blocks due to being at a low frequency; worry, depression, anger, grief are all low energy frequencies and may block a spiritual visit. Spirit is at a much higher frequency than humans and it is far easier for them to communicate to someone who matches their frequency level.

My twin sister had been having a tough time with a friend and although the friend was not being particularly nice to my sister at the time, my sister spent time worrying about her and trying to be there for her. I admire my sister's compassion and empathy, and therefore I supported her choice to continue this friendship, even though I could see this was really draining her. My sister has always had a very close connection to our Grandma in Spirit, whilst I rarely felt Grandma around me; my sister had felt her often. It was a beautiful gift then when Grandma visited me in a dream. My Grandma was a very strong, matter of fact woman and she presented as such in this dream; with a stern face and a firm tone she told me that she was not happy about this friendship and she called this friend a 'dweeb'. I was taken aback when she used this term as I had never heard Grandma use the word 'dweeb' when she was living on earth. As I was waking from this dream, this word was very clear in my mind, it is likely that this word is the very reason that I remember the dream. You must never dismiss a dream or visit from a loved one in Spirit just because they say, do or wear something that does not resonate with what you knew them to be on earth. Spirit will nearly always do this to make the dream/visit memorable, I am always drawn to unfamiliarity in my visits from Spirit and this is what sticks in my mind and helps me to remember the dream. When I shared this with my sister, she was very grateful and said that she had been giving out to Grandma, pleading for her help with this situation. Grandma clearly has a very close connection to my twin sister however, my sister's energy was so drained by this friend that my Grandma could not get through to her directly and so she delivered this message through me. As I type this I can feel the strong bond between my Grandma and my twin sister, and I feel that my Grandma is fiercely protective over my sister; no wonder she has felt frustration by this 'friendship' and felt compelled to intervene and offer some stern words of advice a.k.a *this friend is no good, get rid'*. My Grandma had delivered another message to my sister via me but this time it was delivered in a vision. I was relaxing on my bed when I was transported somewhere else and I was watching my sister preparing to walk into a new world, she knew she had to do this but she was very scared. My sister had not realised that Grandma was standing behind her watching her the whole time, when suddenly my sister gave way and called out to Grandma. Grandma smiled and stepped forward as if she had been patiently waiting for my sister to call on her. My sister felt a huge sigh of relief and found the strength to walk in to this new world and my Grandma walked with her. This really resonated with my sister at that time because of what was going on in her life. My Grandma was simply reminding her that she is right there and my sister must not forget to ask her for help. Our loved ones in Spirit will always try their best to help us, but we have free will and sometimes they are not able to intervene without us asking them to.

Our loved ones in Spirit will be around us the most when we are going through challenging times however because we are at a low frequency, we are not likely to be aware of them. Still they will find creative ways to try to cheer us up. They may put a thought in your head like 'go for a walk', knowing that the fresh air will make you feel better, or they may reach out to your friends and family and put a thought in their head such as 'ask Timmy to meet you for lunch today'. When you randomly think of a friend out of nowhere, it's very likely that Spirit has encouraged that thought and they wish for you to reach out to that friend, either because they need your support or you need their support. I love children, and Spirit encourages me to spend time with my friends who have young children when I am feeling low, this always makes me feel so much happier. Spirit will also encourage you to be kind to a stranger, they may do this by drawing your attention to a stranger who is having a challenging time and for some reason you don't feel you can look away from this stranger without offering help, or you may have a nagging thought to talk to this stranger. My partner and I were travelling to Turkey for a much needed holiday; we were sitting behind a middle aged couple with an excitable three-year-old boy who did not want to rest during the three-and-a-half hour flight, this clearly offended other passengers and the air hostess who spent some time trying to entice the child to sit down, with sweets. I smiled as I could see the light radiating from this child, and then I put my headphones in and didn't take much more notice. On the flight back from the holiday, we were sitting opposite the same people; I felt a slight dread at the pit of my stomach as I registered that this was probably not a coincidence. I am a reserved person and it can be a challenge for me to offer the support Spirit wish me to in such situations, however when I leave the situation without offering the support, I feel heartache and sense of loss and so I have learnt to do as I am guided to do. The middle aged couple were constantly apologising to others on the plane, and I could feel their anxieties as passengers huffed and puffed, whilst they tried so desperately to encourage their child to settle down. I found the courage to offer them a reassuring smile every now and then so they knew this beautiful child was certainly not causing me any harm. I kicked myself as we were leaving the aeroplane, as I could feel that heartache within telling me whatever I was supposed to have done was not done. As my partner and I were waiting to collect our luggage, I noticed that someone had knocked a child's buggy whilst getting their suitcase and it was now half off the carousel; 'someone had better save that buggy' I thought, but I stopped myself from grabbing it for fear that I may not be strong enough to handle it. The buggy fell off on the wrong side of the carousel, and I watched as a gentleman jumped over the carousel to get his child's buggy, which resulted in the carousel stopping and a lot of unhappy people. I felt ashamed as I ignored the nag from Spirit to intervene, especially as it was the family I had been drawn to on the aeroplane. As my partner and I walked back to the car with our luggage, I turned to look behind me and I saw this same family; knowing this was not a coincidence and thankful for the opportunity to do as I was supposed to do, I waited for the family and I told them how beautiful their little boy is, beaming with pride they both thanked me and their child looked up from his buggy with a beautiful big smile. The heartache I felt just moments before was replaced with a feeling of peace and love, as I knew I had offered the light that Spirit had been guiding me to. This may sound very simple, but somehow it was enough to ease this family's discomfort and anxiety following the events of the flight and the carousel. I always ask Spirit to guide and protect the people that they draw me to, and sometimes asking alone is enough for the heartache feeling to go away. If you feel drawn to a stranger or even more so than usual to a family member or a friend, you could ask Spirit to give this person strength, healing and protection; when this request is sent from the heart, from a place of love, it is so much more powerful than we know

Chapter 10

Levels in the Afterlife

My knowledge of the afterlife is still incredibly limited but my spiritual experiences mean I have more insight into it than most. I was taught that there are levels in the afterlife and that my dad is on one of the higher levels, which means that he has almost no identification with form which is why he mostly presents himself through feel. My step-dad is also doing very well in the afterlife, he has worked his way up the levels by guiding and teaching me however, he still has identification with form which is why he always presents with his physical body when he visits me. I had wondered for some time what level I would be on in the afterlife, when Spirit took me into a vision and told me that I am already in the Heaven level. I couldn't see anything around me but I knew that I wasn't on the highest level and so despite what many people may think Heaven is not the highest level, it is just over halfway. I believe the higher levels lead to nothingness; no materialistic form at all but rather just an incredible sense of Being. I also believe they were showing me that Heaven is a state of consciousness and that I can make Heaven on earth if I so wish. Our learning on earth and in the afterlife helps us to work our way up the levels, and every Soul's goal is to get to the highest level which is ultimately God; every Soul wants to be closer to God.

My step-dad first told me about levels in the afterlife in a dream visitation; for a while my step-dad was in a lower level, not what we might call hell, there were lower levels but he wasn't in Heaven either. He explained it to me like this; imagine being in a cabin room with bunk beds and having to share it with someone you don't know; pretty dull and uncomfortable but not unbearable. Whilst he was showing me this and explaining that he has to work his way up the levels, I began to hear a high pitched noise; my step-dad explained that whilst in this level, he will hear that noise every time someone passes away. I don't remember asking why that was but I wish I did because it baffles me to this day. People pass away all the time and so surely they would hear that noise constantly? My step-dad was not a bad person, far from it but he still had some Soul work to do before he was ready to go to Heaven. I believe this Soul work was made up of situations in his life where he lacked compassion for others and so he had to learn that compassion for those beings. This was easily rectifiable for my step-dad but his greatest challenge was his self-punishment; he did not feel worthy of Heaven and he had fears that God would disapprove of his life choices and so my step-dad rejected Heaven and ultimately rejected God. God is very forgiving and He wants nothing more than for us to be with Him, so God will try everything He can to help us to get closer to Him. Mostly we put ourselves in the lower levels, but also our Soul may know that this is where we need to be for some time to learn those lessons we did not learn on earth. During his time in the lower level, my step-dad learnt to forgive himself and accept himself; he learnt to accept himself as a part of God rather than as separate from God.

I don't much entertain the darker realms but they do exist, I have not experienced the darker level but I imagine Spirit will show me at some point for the benefit of my learning, and to share with others. I have had experiences with negative entities; it was during my first awakening when my mental health was very low. My energy was low and so low energy beings were attracted to me. Negative entities cannot stand light, this includes love and gratitude; they cannot stand to be in the same room as high energy frequency. They cower in fear when they are confronted by a Light Being. As I became to understand this I was able to rid myself of this entity very easily but it was a challenge to raise my frequency. It seems this was a test I had to endure as I was eventually told by Spirit that I had 'passed the test'. I guess the test was choosing between love and evil or as I prefer to call it, 'love' and 'not-love'. Not-love can be very luring and very tempting, it attracts us with pleasure; I'm not implying that pleasure is a negative emotion but rather the evil is what we do to get to pleasure; many people are incredibly lured in by sexual, material and financial pleasure that they do not care whom they harm to get to it, causing many innocent beings suffering and pain, and ultimately turning away from their own light and Soul. Sex, materialism and money are not evil, they are wonderful when used for the purpose of love. Sex is a beautiful energetic connection between two people, and it provides the most precious gift; new life. Materialism and money provide warmth, comfort, food and personal growth; many wealthy people work very hard so that they can give their spouses and children a good life and may also use their money to help others less fortunate than themselves; it is a great blessing to have enough finances to be able to help others. Even dwelling on not-love emotions like our sadness, anger or resentment can be very luring because it gives us a sense of entitlement, which gives us a false sense of purpose and security. Again, I am not implying these emotions are wrong, they are a part of the human experience but it is what we do with these emotions that can become evil; low frequency emotions are not supposed to be felt for a life time, they should be experienced temporarily to teach us a lesson, they certainly should not be used as entitlement to harm oneself or another being.

I know how luring these low frequency emotions are because I have experienced the war between love and not-love; I felt myself in the middle of love and not-love and I felt a strong temptation to go to not-love. I was already feeling very low at the time and so I was vulnerable to low frequency energy, I felt that I was entitled to be angry and resentful and I did not want to give that up; choosing love would mean I would have to give up those low frequency emotions and for a moment I thought I would be powerless without them. Love did nothing at all; it was just there being perfectly present, peaceful and all loving whereas not-love put all its energy into convincing me that I wanted to persevere with those feelings of anger, resentment and entitlement. Of course I chose love but it is really quite profound to reflect on how thin that line was. Love does not need to lure anyone or anything in to make it feel more empowered or whole because it is already perfectly at peace, it needs nothing more or nothing less; everything is as it should be at any given moment and therefore love is always complete. Whereas not-love will never be whole because it is greed, it strives for more believing that the more it has, the more powerful it will be; for not-love to become whole it would have to give up its entire existence, it would have to become love.

Evil is not created directly by God however, it is created by God's creation; humankind. By choosing to cling on to low frequency emotions, humankind has created energy so strong that the energy manifests as an entity. Humans are designed to feel low frequency emotions because it teaches us compassion, forgiveness and unconditional love which ultimately help our progression throughout life and the afterlife; there is a place and a purpose for both darkness and light within our lives. Darkness or challenges are not supposed to get us further away from God, they are destined to get us closer to God. When we have experienced depression, anger, resentfulness and other low frequency emotions we are more likely to empathise with other people experiencing these emotions and therefore we are more likely to forgive and show kindness to these people. However, we are only supposed to experience these emotions for the time at which we are to learn the lesson, which is generally not very long. Humankind has become addicted to holding on to low frequency emotions for a number of reasons; the attention we receive after a period of low mood and therefore fear that if we were to get better, we would not receive the same attention; having felt a low frequency emotion for a period of time that it has become a part of a false sense of identity; feeling guilty for letting go of this emotion if it is linked to a bereavement; clinging on to a negative experience because we feel entitled and aspire to get revenge; but mostly low frequency energy is linked to people denying their truth and therefore pretending for the sake of popularity or chasing a false fulfilment such as money, sex, a career etc. and feeling deeply unsatisfied which can manifest as low frequency emotions. Humankind has created wonderful amenities which may serve our spiritual and personal development however we have become so obsessed with physicality, social acceptance, materialism, money, and sexual pleasure that we are creating our own hell.

You see, the war between love and not-love or good and evil, or God and Satan is not outside of us, it is within us; every day we are faced with challenges and within those challenges we choose to react from love or not-love. For example, we choose fear when we lose a job or a relationship, or we choose freedom, excitement and new prospects; we choose to beep our horn and get angry when the traffic is slow, or we choose to turn the radio up, sing a song and have a good time; we choose to berate ourselves for making a mistake, or we choose to laugh it off and forgive ourselves. These are simple scenarios we face every day but whether we choose love or not-love will impact how we meet the next challenge and where this involves another adult, child or animal, it will impact how we respond to that being which may impact how that being responds to their circumstance; angry, sad, scared, loving, kind, resilient etc. I could have chosen to continue to be angry about my dad's death, to blame myself that my step-dad had died and to resent my local general practice with the view that they failed both my dad's. I could have chosen to feel that my life lacks without my dad and step-dad, and that my life is unfair; or I could have chosen purpose, that is to listen to my Truth within, to what my Soul came here to do; to experience these circumstances as a lesson to be learnt, and to choose to allow them to bring me closer to the spark of God within me, which is every Souls purpose. To the Soul the challenges we face on earth are a gift, they are an opportunity for growth, to go up a level and to ultimately get closer to God. The Souls motivation, only desire and purpose is to be with God. I have experienced being in God's presence and the desire to constantly want to go back there and so this gives me a very small insight into the aspiration of the Soul.

Chapter 11

'In Heaven Everything Worships God'

I want to start this chapter by reminding you that **you are God's gift to this earth**, this is how incredibly special you are!

I have experienced God as a separate energy, and I have experienced God as a part of me. I suppose it is like how we inherit our parent's DNA when we are conceived. We inherit some of our parent's qualities and in that sense they are forever a part of us, but we also have our own individual qualities that we have learnt throughout our life experiences. So when God created each and every one of us, we all inherited God's love. We all have that same spark of God within us and that connects all of us, but we also have our individuality which makes each one of us unique. I have experienced the connectedness to all beings. I have been 'a fly on the wall' when someone has received tragic news and in that moment I have felt the emotions off all the people in that room; pain, fear, relief, confusion and yet I have also experienced myself as the observer; as separate from the events but equally as a part of those events. This is how God experiences life, through each and every one of us; so what we say or do to another, we are saying and doing to God. And what we say or do to ourselves, we are saying and doing to God. This can be any mundane action and any mundane emotion; all of it, every single part of it is experienced by God. So in any moment you have to think *'would I do or say that to God'* if the answer is no, then do not do or say that to anyone. Whilst God is experiencing life through us, God is also watching over us and guiding us as a separate energy. God has no attachment to the emotions you are experiencing, so God may be experiencing your fear and sadness whilst also experiencing His own eternal peace and love. God is experiencing all of it simultaneously.

My experiences with God were initially spontaneous and would happen when I was relaxed in the bath or on my bed. Every time I plan to go into a vision, I ask that I am able to have another vision with God however, I don't have anywhere near as many visions with God as I would like to. I don't recognise God by form, I recognise God by how He makes me feel and because I almost always become a child in God's presence. Some people say God's presence is so overwhelming that they have felt frightened however, that is not my experience at all; my experience is of a very gentle, loving energy that has humour. When you have been in God's presence, you really do want to do everything you can to get back there, and you really do want to please Him; not because He tells you to worship Him, in my experience God is very humble but because His love is so incredible that you naturally want to show Him gratitude. Until recently, I didn't even buy into the concept that God created us all individually, but I have since been taught by Spirit that God created every single part of us and that every part of our body has a purpose. To help me understand this, I was shown my fingers typing and as I was typing gold sparkles was coming from my fingers as if they were creating magic. I was told that my gift to the world is my writing. So I understand that the primary purpose of my hands is to write/type but another's hands role may be to spread love by music like playing the piano, for example. Every single person on this earth has a gift to give to the world, a gift that will in some capacity have an impact on humankind and how the universe moves. Everyone has something that makes them a little unique, a little different from the other, this is your gift. Many people say *"I am not special, I am not good at anything; I have no gifts"*. Remember YOU are the gift.

I have heard people say that no one is more special to God than the other because we are all the same to Him, and I've even heard people say that we are insignificant to God. This is not true, God loves us all on a personal level, He created us individually; there isn't a single part of us that is an accident and God loves us each in our own uniqueness. God loves us for our own personality quirks, some we take home to Heaven with us and some we leave behind with our physical body. Although I am not very playful or childlike in human form, when I am in a vision with God, I become playful and childlike and these are qualities that God loves about me.

In Heaven everything worships God; Souls, Angels, plants, trees, rivers, all give thanks to God whatever they are doing, I would say it is like being surrounded by beautiful music all the time but the music is coming from within you to God, and all life that surrounds you is also singing the same song to God; it is as natural to praise God in Heaven as it is to breath here on earth. It is really quite strange that so many of humankind reject God, or shy away from acknowledging His existence (myself included), when acknowledging God and loving Him, is so natural to what we truly are. We think that we could never love any being more than we love our children or spouses, but when we are in the spirit world, we cannot love any being more than we love God. Think of all that love you have for someone significant in your life, times that by one hundred thousand; this is how much your Spirit self loves God. Now times that love by ten thousand, million and beyond; this is how much God loves you. Before we came to earth, we promised God we would never forget His love for us, and our love for Him because in the spirit world, that love is so strong we really did believe we could never forget it, but so many of us do forget it. I used to think the first person I would run to in Heaven would be my dad and if this is what I wish for, this is what God will allow me. But this is no longer my wish, now I know that I will run straight into the arms of God and this is where I will find my dad.

I know that I have already explained early in the book how I communicate with God but I want to share this vision with you and I felt it appropriate to share it at this point in the book; when I asked God how I can explain to people how I communicate with God in my everyday life, He showed me that I should explain it like music; He showed me musical notes coming from the inside and out of me, and I knew those notes represented the communication between God and I. When we listen to a person playing the piano or the saxophone for example, and something within the music evokes certain feelings; happiness, love, excitement. Even though no words are spoken in that, the music is communicating with us through feel; through our *Being.* It is either telling us a story or helping us to relive a story. Even music where words are used, the story will be experienced differently by all people; One hundred people can listen to the same music but we will all hear it differently; it will evoke within us whatever experience best suits our individuality.

Many people have beautiful experiences with Source and choose to cherish it only for themselves; it is enough to give them the hope and strength they need, and they do not want to share it for fear of judgement or other people's opinions making the experience less beautiful. This is perfectly OK, indeed it is not always the case that God and Spirit wish for you to share your experience. However, Spirit has shown me that my experiences must be shared. The concept of writing about God and sharing my experiences of God with other people was initially very frightening for me; I believed people may think I am making it up, or that I am mad, but also because I cannot do God justice, it is something that is felt and is very hard to explain or write about. What I can say is that God loves us so incredibly much and when we begin to acknowledge God and love Him back, it brings Him so much joy. It does not matter what you call God/The Universe/Allah/Higher Source, Him, Her or it, God only asks that we acknowledge His existence with love and acceptance. God loves us to love Him because the more we open our hearts to God the easier it is for Him to guide us to live an authentic life. If you want to thank God for the beauty you have in your life, you can thank Him by being kind, generous, forgiving and loving to all beings, and equally to yourself. Allow yourself that long hot soak in the bath, the 5k run you've been wanting to do for months but haven't had the time, read that book you've been meaning to read; you can thank God by taking the time to do these things for yourself. Remember, what you do to yourself, you do to God. So if you allow yourself to do what brings you joy, you are bringing joy to God. It really is that simple. When I have visions in God's presence, His love is so incredible that I had felt there was nothing that I could do to show Him how grateful I am for His unconditional love, so when Spirit showed me this, and that it really doesn't have to be so grand and extravagant, I was overjoyed and equally, it made perfect sense.

Many people's perception of God is different and for some the connection to God's light within may simply be expressed by an overwhelming feeling of self-love rather than experiencing it as an entity. If you can love yourself and be the best person you can be without inflicting harm on others, then God is overjoyed. We have no place to judge other people's experience of life, or expression of their Truth; it is wrong for a person of religion to judge an atheist and vice versa, everyone's journey is different. There is so much beauty in religion; hope, love, forgiveness and faith that can move mountains; many people find an incredible strength that they would not have without their religion. God loves to be loved and it is so beautiful that religion brings people together to share their love of God; it is most beautiful that religion provides a sacred place where we can pray and sing to God. I know little about any religion but I love that each religion has its own unique connection and experiences of God, and I especially love that religion acknowledges and gives thanks to God. However, some people follow a religion out of fear, believing that if they do not follow a religion they will not go to Heaven; this is simply not true and goes against everything that God is. God is not fear based; God is love. An atheist may be more connected to their Truth and fulfilling their purpose than a person of religion; going to a place of worship for a few hours a week and praising God is not enough, God wants you to be connected to your Truth, and to share His spark of light within you with the world by practicing forgiveness, love, compassion and kindness to all beings. You can share God with the world by being aware of your true essence within; that is God within you. If you can be aware of God within you always, and the guidance Source is constantly giving to you, you will connect to God within the other, no matter who they are; they may not realise it in that moment, but your awareness has sparked the light within them, it is up to them to work with that light – their true essence, and to allow it to step forward. This is when life becomes much more purposeful.

Some people are angry at God; people who have a challenging life may give out to God *'why have you done this to me?'* but remember we choose much of our life path before we come to earth and the Soul knows that every experience is temporary, and therefore does not worry about any challenge but rather looks for the lesson within the circumstance. Despite all I know about God and my Spirit self, I can still be very grumpy and some days I feel sad and helpless or very low in mood. However, I am now much more aware and I am conscious (or regularly reminded by Spirit) not to act on these emotions unconsciously, or to let them consume me. I have an emotion from my childhood that has been coming to surface a lot more during this time; I can't seem to shift it. I could feel it arising one morning just as I was about to meditate; I complained to God about this *'can't you just make it go away'*. Immediately, God took me into a vision where Angels were working in what looked like a factory, they had machines and they were working on this low frequency emotion I was harbouring. God told me without words that they are making something of this emotion, they are making it useful. God is constantly giving; God is constantly unfolding events in our life so that something positive can come from any challenge we experience in life, so that we can learn from the challenge and use it to help others or to help ourselves to be more loving and compassionate. In this vision God was reassuring me that the Angels are already working with me to help me to release this low frequency emotion and to learn from it, even though I feel like they are not.

In incidents of crime and murder, you cannot blame God, though many people do. God did not create crime, murder or hatred, humankind creates those with its free will. God will try to intervene but we have free will to reject His intervention, often these people are so consumed by hatred and aggression that they do not hear God's pleas to stop. Some of humankind has used God's name as an excuse to segregate, and to inflict war, terror, fear and power. God has shown me that when people do not listen to their Truth and continue to inflict suffering in His name, He feels helpless and He feels the pain of all the people inflicting, and all the people being inflicted upon; it is a tragedy. Those who believe in a concept of God and fight with others because their concept of God is different have to think, are they really acting from God's word? Would God ever ask anyone to harm or destroy any of His creation, His children? No, He would not. God's wish is that we all come together, accept our differences, get along and love God from our place of Truth, without judging another's place of Truth. God is within all of us but we all experience Him differently and that is a part of our individual journey. When I first began to have these personal experiences with God, I had expected to feel a pull toward religion however, this has not come to surface; indeed I have less of a desire to follow any one religion. I believe that God would like me to be an example of how we do not need to be religious to have a relationship with God; where our Creator is concerned, there is no one size fits all. God wants us all to have a personal relationship with Him, a relationship that is unique only to us; where we can listen to one another and say *'that's not my experience, but that is yours and that's beautiful because that's your journey and how wonderful that God teaches us all differently, in a way that best meets our individual growth'*. If we consider our relationships with our friends, parents, siblings or children, our interaction with each and every one will be at least a little different. A mother does not interact the same with her seven-year-old child as she does her two-year-old child because they are at different stages of development, they have different preferences, their reactions and responses are different; she will treat each child in a way that best meets their individual needs however, she will love both equally as much. Doesn't that make their relationship with their mother so much more special? Because it is an individual connection, there is no need to fight over the differences because what works between the mother and her two-year-old child, will not work between the mother and her seven-year-old child.

I have been shown that the most important transition humankind must make is to unite; unity is something we are lacking on this earth, we experienced a beautiful stint of unity at the beginning of the Covid-19 lockdown restrictions however this was short lived. Many Souls have been sent to earth to teach unity, true unity is where people of all diversities come together and celebrate their differences. There needs to be more space for people of all different cultures to come together and to share their connection to God, and celebrate each and every one in their uniqueness; and if some of those experiences are similar or the same, that is equally as beautiful but not anymore worthy. The consistent teachings across the board in life and in all religions is to love, to forgive, to be generous, to show compassion and to accept all; if people of all diversities are practicing what the majority preach, then unity is perfectly achievable. The problem is, so many of us preach but do not practice.

Visions With God

My first encounter that I recall with God was when I was two years old. My family and I went to play at our local river, Towns Field. I remember it was a bright summer's day and everyone was happy. My next memory is floating above the water and watching my family in the distance. At some point I must have followed my older siblings into the water whilst my mum was tending to my baby brother. Whilst my body was under the water, my Spirit was being held above the water by beautiful white horses, there was hundreds of them to my left and hundreds to my right and they were running; they were in a hurry, I could feel their urgency and I knew it was for me. Though I was aware of this, I was not disturbed by it; I was in a state of euphoric bliss, I was overwhelmingly peaceful yet ecstatically joyful at the same time. I believe I was basking in God's love and I was experiencing what it feels like to be at one with God. I was surrounded by beautiful Angelic music (as cliché as it sounds) and I am so blessed that I have been allowed to hear this music again since. I could see my family on the sand, they looked much further away than they would have been but I could see them more clearly than if I was standing right next to them, and they were so much brighter and more beautiful than I had ever known them to be. I was conscious when my mum pulled me from the water so she says I must have only been under for seconds; technically, I did not drown. I remember feeling angry when my mum pulled me away from that place. I have never forgotten this experience, though I didn't start questioning it until my mid-twenties; I used to think that this is just what happens when you nearly drown. My family remember this day well because it was so traumatic for them; my mum took her eyes off me for one moment and only found me because she had put me in a sunhat that day and saw my hat floating above the water. My siblings say Mum was cradling me in her arms and crying for hours, but it was not traumatic for me; it was beautiful. I recall my family talking about the incident in my early teens, and we all laughed as I told them that it was a wonderful experience for me because I thought I was flying.

I can't remember exactly when or even what triggered me to question that I may well have drowned that day and that some Higher Source was somehow protecting me; one day I just knew. Sometimes I am given a small glimpse of the bliss I felt in that moment, but never to its full extent. I believe it is too intense and too pure for humankind; humankind is not developed enough to be able to process such intense love. I am still not sure if that anger I felt when my mum pulled me from the water was my own anger at being taken away from that place, or the way this world feels compared to that place. I suspect both. I don't believe this experience or the energy I felt in church when I was eleven years old was a coincidence, I believe they were divinely inspired. I believe God and Spirit set up these events in my life as little reminders of that I truly am, to help to keep me connected to God within me. Perhaps at two years old, we begin to disconnect from our Truth within, we begin to be over influenced by the world, and we forget our abundant, infinite existence. I believe God gave me these experiences in my childhood knowing that I would one day share them with others.

My second experience was the loving energy embrace I felt in church, and my third direct encounter with God was when I was around twenty-eight years old. I have chosen not to share this experience in this book as it is very personal. I would have a few profound visions with God in the space of six months, which I loved to have but I kept them very private. During one of my latter visions where I began to feel familiar with Heaven, I was skipping along a path knowing that I was going to meet God. I was met by a small being who asked if I was going to see 'Him', I said yes, the being was taken aback by this; he was surprised that I was meeting with God and this made me feel a sense of importance. I felt I grew ten feet taller in that moment because I was the 'special one' going to see God. God appeared right in front of me but I could not see any form (or if I could, I can't remember it), I could only feel His energy and hear His words. Though, I could see a small being with wings stood next to God. God guided me to a suitcase, within the suitcase stood Jesus; I knew that was my suitcase and I knew this meant that I was about to embark on a journey where Jesus would become my Guide. I didn't take much notice of Jesus in this vision as I only wanted to be with God and so I said to God *"are you coming?"*, God and the being with him chuckled at my innocence and I was brought out of the vision. As I was coming back, I berated myself for asking such a silly question because of course, God is everywhere. Although I loved to be in God's presence in my dreams and visions, I feared it in my daily life; I knew it was true but I also knew my family and friends were not likely to believe me. I thought that if I fully accepted God's light into my life, I would lose much of my human-ness which possesses qualities that my partner and friends love about me, so I thought they would no longer love me. In one of my earlier visions in God's presence, I was shown God's hand reaching down from the sky and my hand, tiny in comparison, reaching to touch it; then I was shown a white door very slightly ajar, with a beaming white light shining through the crack. To help me understand the vision God said *"I will add in a cell phone for good measure"* and chuckled as He said this. A giant black mobile phone appeared, though it wasn't a modern phone; it was a giant black brick phone. I thought it was strange that God used the term 'cell phone' as I would never use that term, but we know that Spirit will say or do something out of the ordinary to help us remember the visit and so that we do not dismiss it as our own ego or a memory. I soon realised that the light signified my connection to Source and the knowledge I have of the Spirit world, and the cell phone signified my role as the communication between God and earth. Still, I shunned away from this for a long time. Around one year later, during reiki, I envisioned the door fly wide open and the white light beaming out in all its glory but I immediately turned away from it. I kicked myself for not having the courage to fully embrace the light. I have since been shown a hand reaching out to me, I am with two other people who are quivering with fear behind me, I seem to be the courageous one leading the way but still I do not find the courage to take that hand. I was told that if we accept God's spark of light back into our lives, we can heal a thousand hearts and I was shown what would happen if I found the courage to take that hand; I was shown a love chain of thousands of people all linking to me, to that hand, to God. Many times I have awoken through the night by a beaming light shining over me but I have been too afraid to look at it so I kept my eyes tightly closed. Eventually I found the courage to turn over and to look at the light that seemed to guard me whilst I sleep. I often wish I was a good drawer so that I could show people what I am allowed to see, but I could never draw this light; we don't have the colours here. It was a hundred different shades of gold with a tint of silver and I remember wondering why it had points surrounding it, a little like how a child would draw a star. It had a personality and I could feel it was taken aback when I turned around, as if it wasn't expecting me to turn when I did and then it quickly disappeared. I would describe it as a loving mother watching her child sleep, I felt an incredible sense of love, security and peace coming from it and I immediately fell back to sleep. Whilst I do not know what this Light Being is, I have concluded that if love had a physical appearance that would be it.

Whilst I found a peace within when I started to develop a relationship with God, I was also experiencing a dull ache as I tried to resist and ignore this relationship in my day-to-day life. It felt like an internal tug of war; as if there was an invisible rope attached to me and someone was persistently tugging on it whilst I was refusing to let go, and then it developed into emotional pain in my heart and throat area but worst of all was the waves of loss and depression; at times this felt unbearable. I often wonder if I was experiencing a fragment of the pain God feels when His creation, His children deny His existence. When I was first shown that God can feel helpless and sad, I did not believe it as I believed that God is at such a high frequency that He could not feel any low frequency emotions; but indeed, God can feel compassion for His creation. Free will was given to us as a gift from God to allow us to be individual and unique and most importantly, to help us to grow and to learn; it hurts God to see us use His gift to inflict pain, and to completely deny Him who gave us the gift of life and free will. During reiki, Nicki would say to me that there was tonnes of trapped energy in my throat chakra, as if I was dying to say something but I couldn't; I knew this linked to my experiences with God and Spirit and not allowing my true self to come forward. I struggled with the fear of sharing my experiences and potentially losing my relationship with my partner and my friends, or not sharing my experiences and potentially losing my relationship with God. Deep down I always knew that I would suffer far more should I lose the connection to Source; when you have experienced the light and love of God within, life without it is unbearable.

I had never spoken to Nicki about my experiences with God, she is the only person I share most of my spiritual experiences with but I thought even she would think this was too farfetched. Instead I asked God to come to me during reiki. I hadn't expected this to happen so quickly but it happened at my next reiki treatment. Nicki told me that she saw a gold line above my heart area which she associates as the connection to Source; she said that she felt a 'God like' presence, who showed her that I am its child and I am also a part of it but that I was not as connected to it as strongly as I could be. This opened the door of communication and I was so thankful to be able to speak to Nicki about my newfound connection to God. I also asked to be able to have this conversation with other people close to me, and not even one week later I received a telephone call from a person very close to me who spontaneously shared that she had had a beautiful dream of God, most wonderfully God presented as a female. I have since had many unlikely friends tell me that they have had some kind of experience with God/Source. So many people deny God and fear talking about Him but almost all people will reach out to God when they are in times of despair. I have heard people say they do not believe in a God but they have prayed when a relative was very sick, or they themselves were at risk of losing their lives or livelihood. This is because at times of crisis, when we feel we have nothing left, we surrender to our Truth and in those moments we listen to that voice within. Many people experience miracles when they find the courage to ask God for help; somehow the money comes up to pay that bill, our loved one gets better or they do not but somehow we find the strength to get through the loss. God will always answer our prayers, we may not always like the answer but it is always in our highest good and we will realise this when we return to Heaven, and are reminded of the journey our Soul chose to take.

I believe we are all searching for God's unconditional love; humankind is desperate to get back to it, our Spirit feels the absence of God's love and our ego confuses it with physicality. We search for it in relationships, drugs, alcohol, food, money etc., and when we don't find it, we feel at a loss and we go to drastic lengths to find it which may result in substance misuse, depression, anger, anxiety and even suicide. It is so ridiculous really; we look for it frantically in everyone and everything else when all along it is right there, within us. When I am with God in a vision, I feel His love and I miss it terribly when I do not feel it in my daily life. I've read many stories of people who have become depressed after a near death experience because they cannot find that love here on earth that they experienced when they were with God in the spirit world. I can really relate to those feelings, however God will say we can access His love wherever we are because it is everywhere and it is a part of us; we just have to choose it. Mother Teresa devoted her life to helping people who are at a disadvantage due to poverty or sickness, she famously said *'each one of them is Jesus in disguise'* but this does not only apply to people of poverty, this applies to people of wealth, people with addictions, people who are angry; this applies to the helpless animal, the rivers and the trees; every single being is a manifestation of God, whatever you are looking at, if it is a part of the ecosystem, it is a part God. The question I have learnt to ask in any situation, particularly situations where a person is presenting as challenging is *'What is this person here to teach me? What is God trying to teach me?'*

Like all Spirit, God's predominant form of communication is through *feel*, because He has no attachment to form. God showed me that if I listen to that feeling inside of me, I will always be OK. That feeling is inside all of us all the time and it is God; we each have our own little piece of God within. Like our Guardian Angel never leaves us, God never leaves us, not even for a moment. Even though I love to have visions with God, I have learnt that when I am with God in a vision it is not His voice or whatever form He chooses to manifest that is comforting me, it is His presence; it is how God makes me *feel*. This is what God had been trying to teach me; that God is not a form, God is a feeling; to love God without attaching any expectation or form to Him, is to truly love God and is just how God loves us; without expectation. We are taught that there are barriers to communication if one cannot see, speak or hear but this is a limitation humankind has made up, for the most real form of communication is available to all beings if we would only access it more often. You see, there is one thing every being on earth has in common and that is to feel, not physically but to feel at our core; to feel that warm hug from the inside when we are cradled by a care giver and to feel the pain in our chest when we lose someone we love. This feeling binds us together for eternity, to all beings on earth, to our loved ones in Heaven, and to God. If we listen to that feeling within that God showed me, then we will always know what we need to know at any given time because that feeling is God guiding us. **God is our inner compass to navigate us through this lifetime**; this may also be known as our intuition. God does not restrict His love to only some of humankind, God's love is fully available to all and there will be many times throughout your lifetime that God's love will intervene. Try to think about a time when you felt very sad or very scared, perhaps you were at a point of such despair yet somehow you found the strength to get up, wash, go to work, or perhaps you stayed in bed for a few days or months but eventually you found the strength to carry on; perhaps you felt a feeling that everything was going to be OK; a momentary peace, even if it was just for a second. This is God's love, that feeling within is God's way of communicating with you.

I asked God why Angels communicate to humankind on His behalf when I know God communicates with us directly all the time. A few weeks later, Spirit showed me that some people believe in Angels but do not believe in God. So I figured perhaps this is why God has His Angels communicate with us, so that those who do not believe in God can find a different way of communicating with Him and can have some kind of a relationship with Source. I also know from conversations I have had that some people believe God is too mighty, and we are too trivial and therefore we cannot communicate directly with God, so these people communicate to the Angels instead. But I want you to know that all communication is experienced by God, whether you believe it or not, you are constantly in communication with God.

I always ask God to give my partner the experiences He gives me, not because my partner necessarily needs them; my partner is an incredible person, his light shines so bright and he is doing the work God wishes him to do very well, even without him acknowledging God and Spirit on a conscious level. Still, I want my partner to experience God and Spirit so that he can understand my experiences and so I do not need to feel worried about his reaction when I share this book. Spirit say my partner does not need these experiences just yet, and they tell me he will understand me better later in life. It always annoys me when they say this *'it's OK for you'* I think *'you don't need to live it'*. This particular weekend I was in a real grump, I was complaining to God about my life and what made it particularly difficult was that I could not feel God during this time; I felt He had deserted me. I said in my mind *"If you are there, send me a rainbow"*. Hours passed and I never got my rainbow, like a spoilt child, I gave out to God *"See, you're not even listening"*. The following morning, this grump was still lingering. My partner is normally very good at making me laugh and lifting my spirits but even he couldn't help me shift it. My partner persuaded me to get out for a walk with him suggesting I would feel better for it, I reluctantly agreed, moaning that we had better make it quick because I didn't want to be late for the party we were invited to that afternoon. I kept my head down and didn't say much during this walk, drowning in my own sorrows that I didn't even really have to drown in, when my partner stopped and looked ahead of him. *'What is he doing'* I thought. As I approached him he pointed to the sky and said *"Look, there's a rainbow"*. In that moment my grump instantly lifted and I felt God's chuckle ripple from the inside out of me. I smiled the rest of the walk home and I thanked God for showing me that He was indeed listening, but more so that my partner was listening to God in that moment when He told him to stop and point out the rainbow. My partner doesn't appreciate nature as much as I do and it is normally me who stops and marvels at the sky or rainbows, so it was strange in itself that my partner had done this. God was showing me that even though I don't think my partner experiences God and even though my partner may not know it on a conscious level, he does experience God and he listens to God's guidance. God is communicating with us every day, all the time; **we can ask God a hundred questions, God will give us a thousand answers.** God is always finding creative ways to answer our prayers but we so often forget to listen. I am guilty of this myself; I was so absorbed in my self-pity on that day that had my partner not pointed out the rainbow, I likely would have walked straight past it.

We are coming out of the Covid-19 restrictions as I finish typing 'A Father's Love'. I had my second vaccine booked for Friday 3rd September 2021. I was told I may experience flu-like symptoms in the few days that followed, and so I booked it just before the weekend so that I could rest if I was feeling under the weather. I thought I got off lightly when I got in to bed on Friday evening with just mild fatigue, but I was wrong. I awoke at around one a.m. with a temperature; my partner held me tightly as I was viciously shivering uncontrollably. He later joked that he was scared to let go of me encase I shivered out of the bed. I needed to get to the bathroom but I was reluctant to get up; because of my small weight, my blood sugar drops quite quickly when I am poorly, and so I often faint when I try to get up and move around. I was repeatedly praying to God in my mind asking that He would help me to feel better and give me the strength to get to the bathroom. A moment past when I felt God's hand touch the top of my head; that same giant hand that I am so familiar with by now. As God touched my head, I felt Him say without words *"I'm going through it all with you"*. I was reminded that everything I was feeling, God was experiencing too. I was reminded that no matter how sick or scared we feel, we are never going through it alone; God is experiencing all of it with us. I cannot emphasise this enough; **we are never alone, we are never without God.** The shivering stopped for a moment and I found the strength to go to the bathroom and take some paracetamol. I got back in to bed, no longer shivering but scorching hot. As I laid my head down, I noticed that the bedroom was no longer pitch black, there seemed to be a faint light flickering; as if we had a candle burning – *'that light that guards me while I sleep'*, I thought. A familiar calmness came over me and I was finally able to fall back to sleep.

The year 2021 has been very difficult for many people, Covid-19 has caused a collective shift in consciousness and it is happening at lightning speed. We are being forced to face our fears and to overcome mental and emotional blocks. Spirit showed me that this shift would be very difficult for me; they showed me that during this time, I would feel that God had abandoned me and I would fear the transition. In the vision I foresaw my transition and although the end result was beautiful, it was so far removed from what I knew, I resisted it. I said to Spirit that I did not wish to go through this transition because it was so different from the life and body I had become familiar with. Whether I liked it or not, this transition would begin three months later. During this time Spirit would replay the vision in my mind over and over again and every time I would push it to one side. I really complained to God and Spirit a lot during this time. I believed it was all a lie, the world was not beautiful and I was angry that Spirit was trying to teach me that it was when I was witnessing and experiencing so much pain; I felt at a loss and I was losing hope. After a difficult Monday at work, I sat on my bed and I instantly felt God, I breathed a sigh of relief and I set my intention to meditate with God. I have Lorna Byrnes book *'Prayers from Heaven'* by my bed and just before I began meditation, God guided me to open this book and to read the prayer from the page that I opened the book at. The prayer was 'Prayer for Belief' a prayer to help us to believe in God. I was taken aback by this, *"you don't think I believe in you, God"*. I said in my mind, and then I was shown all those times where I felt hopeless and lost and that life was not beautiful. God told me without words, that every time I felt this way; every time I did not believe in myself, I did not believe in God. As much as I am confident that I do believe in God and Spirit and all that they are teaching me, I often doubt myself and God has shown me that my self-doubt impacts my connection to Source and Spirit. My self-doubt has impacted my confidence to share A Father's Love, some days I would try to think up excuses not to share it but I would always feel that dread at the pit of my stomach, that knowing that I am not to keep this knowledge all to myself. During this time, I went for a reiki treatment and as I relaxed on the bed, I was transported to a black space; it wasn't unpleasant at all, it was just pitch black, I would say it was like being in my mind and inside my mind was this black space. God reached out His hand from behind me and pushed me forward, I resisted and I said *"but what if no one believes me"* (my book), God said *"I believe you and there is a piece of me inside everyone. So somewhere inside everyone, there is a part of them that will believe you"*.

As well as my fears that people may doubt my experiences with God and Spirit, I also have worries that people may assume that my experiences and knowledge of God and the spirit world must mean that I am 'gifted' or 'special' or *mad*, but I am no more any of these than you are. We all have that same connection to Source and we are all chosen to come to earth to remind humankind of God within them, and God surrounding them; a God that loves humankind so much. So as you have read this book, you will not have learnt anything that you don't already know, in fact you should find yourself saying *"ah yes"* as that little spark within flares up, and you are reminded of that you truly are.

Jesus

During my spiritual awakening after my step-dad passed away, and before I had any experiences with God and Jesus, I asked my Guardian Angel to teach me how to love unconditionally. This was the beginning of my visions with Jesus.

I was relaxing on my bed when I was transported into an open space; I cannot recall my surroundings as I was fixated on Jesus, who was stood about five steps in front of me. Jesus appeared to be equally as fixated on me. In this vision Jesus allowed me to feel the unconditional love he has for humankind, this was not the love he has in Spirit, this was the love Jesus had for humankind when he was on earth, in human form. This love that I could feel that Jesus has for humankind is so strong, it is an unconditional love that I did not know humankind was capable of. I said to Jesus, *"how can you, as a human being have so much love for humankind?"* Jesus did not answer, he simply smiled.

I do not know how much of what the Bible states about Jesus is true, but I do know that every time I have a vision with Jesus, he is helping to heal me. I also know that Jesus has a very strong connection to planet earth and to humankind. Jesus has the ability to empathise with each and every one of us, and this means he will forgive us instantly because he feels our pain as if it is his own. Jesus has so much compassion for humankind; he understands every choice we make, even when humankind makes terrible choices. Most remarkably, Jesus had this incredible ability to empathise with human beings whilst he was in human form himself.

Jesus longs for humankind to have compassion for one another, so that we can love one another as powerfully as Jesus loves humankind. Jesus has shown me that this unconditional love is achievable here on earth, more so this is why every Soul is sent to earth, to bring this unconditional love, to take it everywhere we go and to pour it into everyone we meet. This is the only way we can make this world a better place; this is the only way we can prevent humankind from destroying itself.

Chapter 12

Thank You

I am constantly reminded of the importance of sharing this book; I see so many people grieving their loved ones who have passed away, people who are in such pain and desperation, it breaks my heart to see. I have such compassion for people who are grieving because I am so familiar with the pain myself; I carried it with me for many years. God loves us so much, it upsets Him to see us suffering, that is why I have been guided to share this book; to share with people that death is not the end and that our loved ones are still around us, their love for us never dies and we will see them again in Heaven. This book is not only for people grieving, it is also meant for people who are nearing the end of their time on this earth, who may be unsure or frightened about what happens next; you really have nothing to fear, you are not alone and you will not be alone when you transition home to Heaven, you will think to yourself *'what was I so worried about'*. More so you will continue to be with your loved ones, to guide them and to protect them; death in itself is a very beautiful experience, it is getting there that is the challenging part. If you are coming to the end of your life on this earth and you fear repercussions in the afterlife for the mistakes you have made, know that you are safe and you are loved; something that God has shown me is that He loves everyone forever, He will never give up on a Soul but we must develop compassion and sorrow for our actions and when we do, we are instantly forgiven by God.

My mum and I had a conversation about the day my dad passed away; the hospital team who worked with my dad became very fond of our family, it was challenging for them to see a young man face death when he had all these children, and a young wife who would be left to fend for six children on her own; it was perceived as cruel and unfair. One of the nurses who cared for Dad called around one morning and offered to take my siblings and me to her farm for the day to give Mum some respite. I remember this day well, we got wet and muddy and we were all cleaned in an outdoor bath tub and there were little yellow ducklings. I remember it feeling like the best day ever, I had so much fun. We had no idea that this would be Dad's last day on earth. We returned home shattered and ready for bed. That night whilst his children were tucked up in bed, Dad would peacefully fall to sleep for the very last time. Mum told me she asked the doctor if there was any way they could bring him back, she told me the doctor cried. Later that day Mum went for a walk and suddenly she was consumed by an overwhelming feeling of relief and peace, as if a great burden had been lifted, and she spontaneously said out loud *"thank God I'm alive"*. Mum told me she has never understood why this happened and why she said those words, she even insinuated that she felt guilty for it. I told Mum that perhaps this was Dad; finally he was free from the burdens of his illness, he was at peace and he was giving thanks because indeed, he was still alive beyond his physical form; most importantly, he would still be able to watch his children grow. Mum accepted this and said she had never thought about it like that. I enjoyed this conversation with Mum; I wanted to know every detail. Even with my awareness and my connection to Dad, I felt the lump in my throat as Mum shared the details of his final hours on this earth, but I did not feel sad, I felt joy. I knew that it would be very difficult for my mum to have this conversation with any of my siblings as they may become emotionally overwhelmed, but I was so very grateful for it and I knew it was an important part of her healing. I knew this because the following morning I awoke to a gentle breeze on my left ear, I kept my eyes closed and I said in my mind *"I know it's you Dad because you're my left side"*, and then I felt him say *"thank you"*.

They Never Really Leave Us

I was relaxing on my bed on a cold winter's afternoon, when I was transported into a vision; I was a child again looking at a long dark path, surrounded by stars. I looked to my left and my dad was standing next to me, he told me I had to walk the path but when I asked if he could walk it with me, he said *"No, but I will be right here waiting for you"*.

We can choose to believe that death is loss and tragic, or we can choose to believe that death is simply a short time away from one another, a time where our journeys had to be on different paths but along the way, eventually the paths will realign and we will be together again. My dad is not physically here but his love for me never left and my relationship with him is stronger than ever; it is the most beautiful relationship because it is based on faith, trust and unconditional love, not physicality. As humans we rely on physical so much but there is no truth to physicality, there is truth in feeling something so deep that you know it's real, even though you can't see it or hear it. We make the most honest decisions and judgements based on how we feel, so why don't we believe in it? We tend to call it coincidence or imagination.

Everyone has the ability to feel their loved ones in Spirit; it's the wind brushing past your hair when there is no breeze, the shivers down your back, the gentle tug on your arm, the tingles on the top of your head or simply knowing someone else is in the room with you when you should be alone; and then it's the feather floating down at your feet, the light flickering even though there is no electric fault and the song that reminds you of them playing on the radio at just the right time. When you start to acknowledge these, a portal is opened, there is a shift in energy and a connection begins; that's when the magic really starts to happen.

Death doesn't have to be a tragedy because you see, there is no such thing as loss; they never really leave us.

'Like moonlight on the water, and sunlight in the sky,
fathers and daughters never say goodbye'

Epilogue

In loving memory of my dad, William (Billy) Charles Houghton (1953 - 1996); my big star, forever by my side, forever in my heart. We have a bond not many understand, but we know it to be true.

In loving memory of my step-dad, Kenneth John Hind (1945 - 2017); my guiding light, I am blessed and thankful for every moment we continue to spend together, and all that you are teaching me.

In loving memory of my Grandad, my first love, and my Grandma; precious memories, forever cherished.

Printed in Great Britain
by Amazon

83786841R00119